Stars in Their Own Write

Stars in Their Own Write

Derek Holmes

 **Robson Books**

First published in Great Britain in 1989 by Robson Books Ltd,
Bolsover House, 5–6 Clipstone Street, London W1P 7EB

British Library Cataloguing in Publication Data
Holmes, Derek
Stars in their own write.
1. Graphology
I. Title
155.2'82
ISBN 0 86051 590 7

Typeset by Selectmove Ltd, London
Printed in Great Britain by Biddles Ltd
Guildford and King's Lynn

'In every man's writings, the
character of the writer must
be recorded.'
Thomas Carlyle, *Goethe*

Contents

Introduction

The main purpose of this book is to entertain the reader by providing an insight into the behavioural characteristics of many famous personalities from the fields of stage, screen, television, radio, journalism and sport. If you ever wonder what it is that activates such people as Sir John Mills, Roy Castle, Auberon Waugh and Sir Alastair Burnet, then wonder no more. You will find the main ingredients of their personalities laid bare within the covers of this book by the means of graphology, the study of character through the analysis of handwriting.

To make the contents of this book even more meaningful and entertaining you could try and discover for yourself the thread or threads which link some or all of the personalities you admire. Is it imagination, creativity, the ability to communicate, strength of character or sensitivity, or is it a combination of two or more of these qualities? Fame is an elusive beast and it might bestow its favours on only one in a thousand even if they all are endowed with equal talent. There is a school of thought among psychologists which believes that a person who is sufficiently charismatic will be able to ensnare the hearts and minds of thousands or even millions of others by casting their persona over them in much the same way that a Roman gladiator would cast his net over his hapless victims. There are in the world many ex-teachers with a literary bent, but there was only one Arthur Marshall.

Equally, it can be said that actors abound whilst few have the qualities that make Sir John Gielgud so well loved and respected. How many boxers have earned a place in the hearts of their thousands of followers to the extent of Henry Cooper? Why are the books written by Barbara Cartland read by so many? What quality does she introduce into them that is so hungrily sought after by her millions of readers? Everyone that is represented in this book has achieved fame to the point where they have become household names. Why is this, and what is the common link that attracts to them their massive following of tens of thousands of their fellow citizens? Somewhere, buried deep in their personalities there must be a characteristic which is common to each, and when this is combined with a natural aptitude that is present in sufficient quantity, it is able to command the affection and respect of others on a large scale. What then is the common denominator, the feature that makes fame and fortune smile upon them?

When you have read all the character profiles you will discover that some of those analysed appear to have the ability to relax, even under the most stressful conditions. Others appear to move always under tension, burning up their nervous energy as they go, even when they are at home with their families. Some are strong and capable, whilst others are weak and impressionable, and a lack of psychic balance is evident amongst a small proportion. One or two have wildly fluctuating emotions that could lead them into problems concerning their relationships with members of the opposite gender, but mostly the impulses are stable and this provides them with a well-balanced outlook on life. Many are highly intelligent, but some are not so gifted and they have to compensate with a proportionate increase in shrewdness and cunning. There are the fussy perfectionists, the fluently expressive and those who have to struggle mightily to make themselves understood.

Outspokenness in some is more than matched by the timidity of others, and lack of pretension among those who live well with their fellows is more than compensated for by the ostentation of those who still have something to prove.

Many have found a degree of security in the face of changing circumstances, whilst a corresponding number are plagued by uncertainties and insecurities, although in the main, they do manage to keep their doubts and fears well hidden from the gaze of their public.

Certainly, the opening-up of the personalities of the famous reveals their inadequacies, and proves that in spite of the face they present to the contrary, they are moulded from the same clay that has been used to make us all. Nevertheless, it must be recognized that they are famous and we are not, so in there, somewhere, is there a psychological philosopher's stone that is capable of changing the base metal of ordinary people into the gold of the famous? Keep on reading and examining the profiles, for if you find the catalyst, fame could be yours for the asking.

About Graphology

Graphology, according to one dictionary definition, is 'the study, or art, of inferring character from handwriting', and its elementary principles were known and understood many thousands of years ago. Books have been written on the subject since the seventeenth century and it was in the nineteenth century that the famous French graphologist J. Crépieux Jamin wrote the first book dealing formally and methodically with the subject, outlining for the first time what is now a cardinal rule: that handwriting must be studied as a whole and not just as a number of isolated features.

Handwriting has also been termed brainwriting, as each and every action required to form letters begins with an impulse from the brain. Without these commands the pen could not even be picked up and held, let alone used to construct the complex lines and curves which together comprise handwriting. If the impulses never varied then a person's writing would always be the same, but the mind is affected by feelings of fear, love, excitement, hatred, tiredness and elation, among many others, and those feelings are transmitted to the fingers holding the pen. Check your own writing at different times of the day and you will find that just after you awaken from your night's rest your writing will be different from that which you pen just before going to bed after a tiring day's work. Similarly, a person's state of mind is reflected in their handwriting. You would not expect a confident man to walk with the same gait as a frightened and timid person. Confidence breeds a brisk approach, jaunty and on the balls of the feet, whilst timidity can be shown by a scurrying nervous walk, with shoulders hunched. Granted some of the characteristics of one can be attributed to the other, but not all of them and that is why J. Crépieux Jamin's first principle — that no feature of a handwriting should be taken in isolation — is so important.

To compose a personality profile from handwriting is not unlike painting a portrait. First, the features have to be isolated and given meaning, and then they have to be reconstructed in such a way as to make the dominant parts lead. The less dominant features are then fitted in in such a way as to create a recognizable whole. As with a photograph it is not necessary to show each and every blemish on the skin to make someone recognizable, so with handwriting it is not necessary to reveal each and every psychological blemish if all one wishes to do is to make a profile recognizable and interesting.

As the periphery nuances of a particular script can change if the person doing the writing is tired, or has, for instance, suffered a shock, it would seem that the analysis of a handwriting can only apply to the circumstances prevailing at the time of writing. Whilst this is true in a general sense, it is rare for the fundamental features of a writing to change markedly, and it is those fundamentals which have been studied to produce the personality profiles in this book. There are forty or so fundamentals that need to be studied, enabling variations of the writing from the school model to be isolated and interpretations placed upon them. Once the interpretations have been made the features that are dominant are placed together and the other items which are not so strongly indicated are fitted around them.

The Important Features of Analysis

In the following pages I describe the key features of handwriting which, with the main characteristics identified in the handwriting of each personality analysed in this book, will help you to gain a better understanding of graphology and, through that, of yourself and others. When you examine a handwriting, try, as I have in this chapter, to relate at least a part of it to one of the analysed scripts of the famous. Look for variations as outlined and then compare them with the explanations given.

Whilst there are approximately forty deviations from the school model of handwriting which need to be minutely examined when making an in-depth analysis, it is only necessary to examine eleven of them to obtain a fairly good idea of what a person is really like. I will now guide you through those eleven and provide sufficient information to let you create your own personality portraits of individuals.

Before you begin any analysis there are three things you need to know about the subject. The first is the sex of the person whose script you are examining, as to date no way of defining gender through handwriting has been discovered. This is not so surprising if one accepts the fact that both male and female characteristics reside within us all. The second piece of information you must have is whether the writer is right- or left-handed. It is important to know this when checking the slope of the letter strokes, for a reason which will be given later. The third and final detail you should have is the approximate age of the person, as I have seen very vigorous writing come from the pens of some elderly people, and weak and tremulous strokes from the young. Examples in this book of strong writing emanating from older people are those of Thora Hird (page 62) and John Arlott (page 77).

Once you have this information and a sample of handwriting, begin your analysis by reading through the following guide. To help you better understand what it is you are looking for I have referred you in each case to one or more samples of the handwriting of the celebrities dealt with in this book. Remember that no one feature taken in isolation will tell you what a person is really like, for, just as a photograph of your nose only will not make you easily recognizable, neither will one aspect of your personality reveal the real you.

Always start by assessing the form standard, as this enables you to decide whether the character traits you discover should be given a positive or negative interpretation. For example, heavy pressure in writing of a high form standard would indicate forceful energy which the writer uses purposefully. The same pressure in writing of a low form standard could point to the person channelling that same energy into purposeless aggression.

1 FORM STANDARD

Form standard is the overall impression you receive of a writing when you first view it. When the standard is high, the script is original and fluently simplified or enriched. Layout should be good, with regular spacing between words and lines. In general, the writing appears harmonious and pleasant to look at — writing of a very high standard gives the impression of a work of art.

Low form standard is best described as being untidy in layout, with letters tangling with those of the lines above and below. Individual letters are laboriously formed and in most cases vary little from those taught at school.

Form standard is not a reflection of educational or cultural achievement, rather it mirrors the inherent intellectual and creative potential of a person. Therefore, just as people range in their basic capabilities from the brilliantly creative to those who have progressed barely beyond the elementary, so too does their handwriting.

An example of a good form standard of enriched writing is that of Frank Muir (page 206), whilst a high form standard of simplified script is revealed by Barbara Cartland (page 242).

There is no low form standard writing within this book as the examples are from people who, obviously, possess good intellectual capacity in order to have succeeded in their careers.

2 THE ZONES

At school we are all taught to write in an almost identical manner and whilst there are slight variations from area to area, nevertheless the basics are the same and similar to the following:

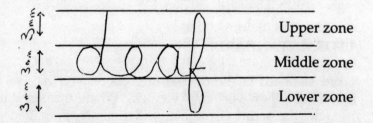

The writing, as you can see, is equally balanced between the upper, middle and lower zones, and there is a moderate leaning or slope of the strokes to the right.

The upper zone is representative of the intellectual and spiritual parts of a person and when this zone is larger and more dominant than the others one should look for these qualities to be at the core of the writer's character.

The middle zone represents the centre of a person's being and is the link between the intellectual and instinctive spheres. It is a barometer of sociability and the desire to live each day fully. When dominant it means that the social, everyday life of the writer assumes an unusual importance.

The lower zone is representative of instinctive desires and primitive sexual and materialistic urges. Long lower loops are indicative of a desire for sexual satisfaction.

If you examine the handwriting of Barbara Windsor (page 228) you will see a perfect example of middle zone domination, and from this feature we can safely assume that she is a very sociable and outgoing person whose everyday life is extremely important to her. Whilst other features in the writing might modify this trait in some way they cannot eliminate this basic personality trait. Una Stubbs (page 231) also has a dominant middle zone, yet while she is also a sociable person, the angular awkwardness of the writing suggests a limit to her adaptability. There are many such counter-dominants to be found in graphology, but their sheer scale and complexity takes them outside the scope of this chapter.

The tall upper zone of Jean Rook's writing (page 27) tells of her intellectualism and of her desire to make something of her dreams — the strokes, which really soar into the upper reaches, are a perfect example of this quality.

Roy Hudd (page 98), with his long swinging lower loops, personifies materialism and a strong instinctive drive.

3 LEGIBILITY

Because handwriting is a means of communication, it follows that from the legibility of both letters and words we can judge quite accurately how much a person desires to have contact with others. Legibility in graphological terms means that all letters and words, taken in or out of context, must be clearly and easily understood.

The handwriting of Thora Hird (page 62) typifies the clearly readable type of writing. From this, we can infer that she is considerate towards others, her general attitude as thoughtful towards them as it is towards the formation of her letters. She has no desire to hide behind the ambiguity of writing in such a way that many words might be read as almost anything.

Auberon Waugh (page 156) and Jonathan Dimbleby (page 144), on the other hand, pay scant regard to how their writing appears to others, and, indeed, to whether or not they can be understood. We can deduce from this that they are awkward men who have no desire whatsoever to meet the world halfway if that should mean they would have to compromise their style and originality.

The above analyses apply because the form standard in each case is high. If it was otherwise then very legible handwriting would be representative of a rather dull person who has little creativity in their make-up, while an illegible script would be that of a careless, untidy-minded individual.

4 LAYOUT

When you look at a page of someone's handwriting you quite naturally make a subconscious assessment of whether or not it is neat, lopsided in some way, carelessly or carefully assembled. To write in an orderly fashion continuously, for line after line, requires skills of co-ordination, concentration and diligence on the part of the writer. Anyone who can write in this way will almost certainly be able to apply these qualities to their general work and leisure activities.

A perfect example of orderly writing exemplifying an equally orderly mind is that of Frank Muir on page 206.

Although there are no illustrations of untidy layout, perhaps the worst is that of Terry Scott (page 46) and this reflects his somewhat erratic and up-and-down personality.

5 SIZE OF MIDDLE ZONE

This is an important feature of graphology as it measures the reserve or otherwise of the writer. A middle zone that is 2mm or less in height indicates a writer who is reserved and the smaller the writing the greater is the reserve. People who write in this way rarely experience violent or passionate emotions and are therefore able to be impartial in their attitude towards events and situations. The ability to concentrate on detail is often another characteristic of such people.

Smallness is a feature of the handwriting of Sir John Gielgud (page 191) and Roy Kinnear (page 184).

The middle zone of Roy Castle (page 235) is a fairly constant 3mm tall, and this medium height is indicative of someone with a well-balanced mind and a realistic approach to life.

A large middle zone of 4mm or more as that of Oliver Reed (page 33) reveals generosity of spirit, broadmindedness and a joy of action and enterprise. If the writing was much taller than this, though, it would indicate some megalomania present in the person. All the specimens in this book, however, are smaller in size than their originals.

6 THE WRITING ANGLE

Does the writing slope to the left, to the right, or is it upright? The angle of the writing is a very useful way of assessing the emotional reaction of the writer to his environment.

The rightward slope is used by the extrovert who has a zest for, and a love of, life and takes great pleasure in being with people. This feature is well illustrated in the writing of Derek Nimmo (page 148).

The upright script of Derek Jameson (page 87) portrays to perfection the independent spirit of the man.

Leftward slopes are featured in the writing of those who are repressed in some way, or those who look to the past for comfort, so it is hardly surprising that in a book full of entertainers it cannot be found.

Look for slope variations in each of the three zones and relate what it is I have explained about them to the instinctive, social or intellectual areas of the writer's life. For example, a slope to the right in the middle and upper zones with a slope to the left in the lower zone would indicate a person who is spiritually and socially directed towards the outside world and the future, but whose instinctive feelings, those that are below the threshold of consciousness, are turned inwards and to the past.

If a person is left-handed then it is quite normal for them to write with a left slope of a few degrees and this has to be taken into consideration. Therefore an upright angle that has been written by a left-handed person is really indicative of a gentle slope to the right with all that that implies.

7 FORMS OF CONNECTION

The three most important forms of connection are:

Garland

Arcade

Angular

A firmly drawn garland, as in the writing of Richard Briers (page 224), Robert Robinson (page 167) and Sir Harry Secombe (page 58), points to kindness and a readiness to help others.

The arcades of John Timpson (page 113) and Sir John Mills (page 65) clearly show that they are men who consider form and deportment to be essential features of their lives and that emotionally they tend to be somewhat detached from those around them.

The angles of Una Stubbs (page 231) reveal her toughness and the fact that she does not shirk her responsibilities but meets them head on.

8 PRESSURE

By measuring pressure the graphologist is able to determine the nature and amount of energy available to a writer. There is a definite relationship between the amount of pressure exerted on the paper and the desire on the part of the writer for activity and the extent of his or her endurance.

The light pressure writing of Willie Rushton (page 140) indicates sensitivity and a desire to avoid unnecessary friction. Usually these people have poor physical appetites.

The medium pressure applied by Michael Aspel (page 55) mirrors vitality and his well-balanced and uncomplicated personality.

The forceful heavy pressure of Henry Cooper (page 91) is no more than one would expect from someone who so obviously knows how best to direct his strong volitional energy.

Irregular pressure patterns — easily detected by turning the writing upside-down — often indicate the coercive nature of a writer, and the fact that while they might be dominantly calm they can fly into a rage for no easily discernible reason. Pressure variations may be seen in the handwriting of Julian Lloyd Webber (page 84).

Quite often, intensity of pressure can best be judged by turning over the paper to reveal the presence or otherwise of ridges caused by the point of the pen. For you to assess the amount of effort needed to make such an indentation is a simple matter, all that is required being for you to exert various levels of force on the paper in question with a pen.

9 SIGNATURE

The signature is a personal flag flown at the end of a letter or other document when a writer wishes to add authority to the contents.

If it is large like that of Barbara Cartland (page 242), it shows pride in the family name as well as in her achievements. See how the capital letters of her forename and surname cover all three zones of the writing. This indicates that she has a real understanding of human nature and what it is that makes people tick.

When small, and similar to that of Kathy Staff (page 120), it reveals moderation and a modest approach to all aspects of life.

If illegible, as written by David Jacobs (page 137), it shows that ambiguity plays no small part in the signatory's dealings with others. The fact is that anyone who signs their name in such a fashion enjoys playing their cards close to their chest.

When, as on page 103, the signature is written in a style that is identical to the main body of the writing, it clearly states that the writer, in this instance Marjorie Proops, is an unpretentious person who prefers forthright relationships in both her social and working lives.

The forename and surname of June Whitfield (Page 126) are perfectly balanced as regards letter size and slant, and this reveals that she manages to keep an equipoise between her private and public lives by giving prominence to neither.

10 LETTER FORMATION

If letters that should be circular are misshapen or distorted in some way, as in the handwriting of David Hamilton (page 42), it indicates a degree of strain or nerve trouble present.

The smoothly formed shapes of Sue Lawley (page 19), on the other hand, clearly show that her emotional impulses are kept on a tight rein and not allowed to interfere with her life.

11 T BARS

Basically there are two types of bars used to cross the letter 't': strong and firm like those used by Jimmy Savile (page 80) and Sue Lawley (page 19), and weak and rather hairlike as used by David Hamilton (page 42).

Those who cross their t's with strongly emphasized strokes are the purposeful people who are not easily swayed by new ideas or situations. Weak crossings suggest the opposite.

MISCELLANEOUS

These items, whilst in themselves not representing a specific graphological feature, can nevertheless assist with an analysis by providing 'filler' information.

Capital letters that appear consistently in the middle of words as in the writing of Jimmy Greaves (page 37) are representative of a natural physical prowess and are often to be found in the script of leading sportsmen.

The lyric letter 'd', which has its upper zone stroke arching to the left as in the writing of Ralph Hammond Innes (page 176) and Sir John Gielgud (page 191), is often to be found in the handwriting of poets and writers. Because this feature is situated in the intellectual reaches of the script it is indicative of the reflective mind.

When combined with good form standard, the omitting of the dot from over the letter 'i' reveals a truly independent spirit, and nowhere is this better illustrated than in the writing of Keith Waterhouse on page 171.

When the forename and surname are joined and written as one word, as in the case of Sir John Mills (page 65), we know that we are reading the writing of a distinctive and individual person. You will notice that this is also a feature of the signature of his wife, Lady Mills.

When a signature is very large like Jean Rook's, on page 27, it is safe to assume that the ego of the writer is easily bruised.

Flamboyant writing such as that of Marjorie Proops (page 103) certainly points to an equally flamboyant personality that is inclined to gild the lily when relating to others.

Wavy bars carefully placed on the letter 't', as executed by Thora Hird (page 62), are a sure sign of the writer having a sense of fun.

Tiny hooks that appear at the end of many strokes indicate quite clearly the tenacity and nervous energy of people like Charlie Chester (page 180).

COMPOSING THE PROFILE

As you extract the relevant information from the handwriting, put your findings down on paper and when you have completed your examination, group together what you have discovered about intellect, creativity, imagination, etc. Then collate the items concerned with emotions and sensations before finally listing separately those additional bits of information that do not fit into any of these categories.

Read your list of discoveries through a number of times, and gradually a picture will emerge of what the writer is like. Write and rewrite the profile until you are satisfied that your final composition contains all the elements found in the analysis.

Work only from the facts and do not allow yourself to guess at any characteristic that has not emerged from the writing.

Start with the handwriting of someone you know well and ask them to give you an honest assessment of your finished profile. As you gain confidence your next step can be to obtain from friends or relatives the handwriting of someone known to them but not to yourself.

There are many books on graphology that will enable you to take your interest further, but it should be stated that to become a competent, professional graphologist you must study under an experienced handwriting analyst as there is no way you can become skilled without tuition other than from books. Nevertheless, it is possible to learn enough from this and other books to be able to take apart a character in general terms and to find out at least something of what makes a person tick.

Ambition

The handwriting that depicts this particular trait is always bold and of a high form standard. The strokes are strong in outline, not at all frayed at the edges, and they slope to the right or are upright. The letter 't' is always crossed with determination and quite often, but not always, the bar points downward.

Sue Lawley

Dear Mr. Holmes ———

     Many apologies for not replying to you sooner! Here are my few lines of hand-writing as you request. Inevitably, I find, one is rather self-conscious when one is aware the writing itself, rather, than the content, is going to be analysed.

     By the by, I am right-handed.

     Best wishes ———

Sue Lawley

HANDWRITING HIGHLIGHTS

The large writing and even size of the middle zone points to the self-confidence of the writer, and the fullness of the letters 'a' and 'o' clearly show her warmth towards others. The understrokes of the letters 'y' and 'g', which remain open to the left, reveal an instinctive perception of the past, while the way in which many letters touch, or become part of the preceding or following letter, suggests that she keeps part of her life away from prying eyes. Strong bars to the 't's indicate her strength of character, and the many letters that are not joined to their neighbour are a sign of her intuitive qualities.

The legible writing, combined with a signature that is identical to the main body of the text, clearly shows that we are dealing with a sincere person who is without pretension of any sort.

PORTRAIT

Sue Lawley is motivated by a strong compulsion to attain her goals and objectives, and by a powerful drive to be successful in whatever she attempts. She does not consider problems to be problems at all, rather they are viewed as challenges to her ingenuity, which have to be overcome as quickly as possible. She is a front runner, delighting in competition, which spurs her on to greater efforts, and she thrives on action, striving continually to turn her aspirations into successful reality. She takes chances to achieve success, and will readily accept responsibility for any mistakes which she considers are of her own making. This she is able to do because of her feeling that she has above-average ability to cope with the daily challenges of life. Although good progress has been made, there are still things left for her to accomplish, and this need for constant achievement means that there must at times be some insensitivity towards the needs of others.

Her mind is often reflective, with an instinctive perception of the past, and there is some conflict between her desire to push forward and explore new fields and her need for security. These uncertainties, while being real, are nevertheless kept well hidden, as she has strength of purpose and is not easily deflected by the opinions of others. However friendly she might appear, it is rare for her to demonstrate her innermost feelings. Her ego is healthy, and she is further blessed with good judgement regarding everyday matters, which enables her to come to terms with any difficulties she might experience.

Cool, collected and very much preoccupied with the present, she rarely, if ever, daydreams, and is rather indifferent to values outside the rational and social world. Her outlook is fairly well balanced, as is her viewpoint; she has a sense of her accomplishment, but with her feet so firmly planted on the ground, she remains natural and unpretentious. Whether in the public eye or quietly entertaining friends at home she has no inclination to act differently, but she does tend to protect her private life, though not enough to put it out of balance with her professional obligations.

Highly intuitive and well able to assess a given situation without having first to give it too much conscious thought, she is a socially helpful person with a readiness to support others, although there is little sentimentality in her make-up. Her mind is clear and original and she is particularly well adapted to the conditions of her work, being fond of people, warm-hearted and having a sense of fun. There is a desire for physical activity and a nervous energy which comes from her imagination, making her appear rather tense, somewhat talkative and definitely unable to relax easily. Earnest and self-critical, Sue Lawley has a need to express herself and this she does through her cultural and literary interests.

She is fortunate enough to have that happy combination of imagination and intelligence which enables her to fulfil her dreams.

'For the most part it was quite uncannily accurate' — Sue Lawley

Steve Ovett

Dear Derek,

Please find enclosed a few words as requested for your study of graphology.

I am left handed.

I look forward to hearing from you!

Regards.

Steve Ovett

HANDWRITING HIGHLIGHTS

Pride can be seen in the flourishes that decorate much of the writing, and in particular this is evident in the signature. Upper and lower loops are full, indicating an active imagination; the middle zone is also very round, revealing a warm and caring disposition. The writing is quite large and there is about it a certainty of aim that points to strength of character and a love of action and enterprise. The letters 't', 'h' and 'l' are started at the top by a stroke coming from the previous letter. This is a sure sign of the intellectual extrovert. The general flow of the letter strokes is indicative of rhythm and co-ordination, and the strength of the bars crossing the letters 't' state that here is a man who is not easily deflected from his chosen course of action. Although his signature is not clearly readable, the first and second names are well balanced and from this we can assume that his private and public lives are harmoniously integrated. It is on the left side of the body of the writing, which shows some reserve in the personality, whilst the overall upright nature of the letters provides an insight into the control that he applies across the whole spectrum of his affairs.

PORTRAIT

Steve Ovett is a man driven by a deep longing to make something of his dreams, and whose depth of intellect makes possible an enthusiastic development of opportunity. His mature mind is ever open to new ideas and seeking new worlds to conquer; his interests and ambitions are numerous and divergent, and because of the planning and forethought he puts into his actions he is able to proceed on the basis of reality rather than losing himself in wild speculation. He will, however, act independently and depart from the well-trodden paths to express ideas that are novel and unusual; yet those ideas are soundly based and more often than not they are workable, for the happy mixture of imagination and intelligence bring reality to the visions.

His general outlook is independent, and his nature self-reliant, and whilst he is normally calm and reliable, he can on occasion be moody, argumentative and downright unsociable. The reason for this departure from his basic personality structure is the egotism, the pride and the outspokenness that also form a part of his character. He is usually clinical in his relationships with others as he fears that getting too close, certainly in the early stages, might make him lose some of his dignity. Therefore, even though he is friendly, initially he is guarded and unwilling to let himself go. In spite of this, he is, with those he knows well and likes, forthcoming and spontaneous, but even here, although he will quite happily reveal his thoughts, he will not lay bare his soul; he is well able to combine frankness with keeping his own counsel.

He has perseverance and endurance and is able to work hard at an appointed task, using all his qualities in the fulfilment of his aims. There is a desire for activity and he is obviously accomplished in physical skills but he is not too keen on routine and prefers to keep moving as he becomes stifled when confined to one place for too long.

He is a gentle person — certainly not aggressive — and his agile mind tries always to avoid unnecessary friction. Aestheticism, idealism and intellectualism are all in his make-up, and he can enjoy and appreciate both art and literature. There is some exaggeration of ideas as he enjoys his imaginative experiences, but he does understand that this *naïveté* has to be controlled if he is to prevent it becoming too dominant a feature of his life. Because of this self-knowledge and the fact that he can apply a strong personal control he is not swayed too easily by new ideas and untried situations. He is still influenced and inhibited to some extent by the past, but his disciplined defence against this has resulted in a strong sense of purpose.

He has a healthy physical appetite, and his desire for activity is greater than for reflection — so much so that he does at times react so quickly to a particular situation that he appears not to have exercised any judgement at all.

With his joy of action and enterprise he is mostly inspired to act in a positive and definite manner and he has complete confidence in this inspiration. The attendant feelings of accomplishment are strong. Although his private and public lives are kept apart, they are nevertheless in balance as he tries not to become too dependent upon public acclaim for satisfaction; he does, however, feel a need to impress.

He is sincere, and considerate of the needs of others, and being an honest man he does not feel it necessary to twist, veil or distort facts. He has adjusted to the world and has a sense of order, rhythm and co-ordination. His thinking is clear and unambiguous and he is well adapted to work, social life and circumstances.

Whatever Steve Ovett might have achieved, it would be safe to assume that there is more . . . much more . . . yet to come.

Jean Rook

My handwriting is so appalling,
I hesitate to send it. I keep
meaning to make my " t " come off
the top (like that) because it
looks more exotic but I always
forget

Jean Rook

HANDWRITING HIGHLIGHTS

Extended lines which travel well into the upper zone indicate intellectualism and a wish to make something of her
dreams. The illegibility of the writing in general clearly
shows that she does not court popularity and that she
can be hostile towards the demands made on her by her
environment. Many final letters of words are taller and

this means frankness, a readiness to defend her views, arrogance and a lack of sensitivity. Lack of rhythm in the writing points to excitability, and blunt finals clearly show the unyielding side of her nature. The irregular nature of the writing reveals a never resting mind unfettered by acquired form and tradition. The vigorous underlining of the name clearly displays her unconscious desire for greatness, importance and fame, and the bloated loops in the name capitals indicate that, if necessary, she will gild the lily in order to win recognition. The broad pasty strokes – strokes of even width – of the writing are those of a warm sensual person who lives and relies on her senses; a human being, near to life and nature. Thick pasty strokes are made by a long hold on the pen and point to a personality that flows with the tide of life rather than one that fights against it. Strong bars crossing the letters 't' denote pugnacity and a quarrelsome tendency.

PORTRAIT

There emerges from the handwriting of Jean Rook a personality so powerful, so turbulent that it is hardly surprising its owner has earned the title of 'First Lady of Fleet Street'.

She possesses considerable mental agility and her never resting mind exercises its ingenuity by continuous intellectual exploration and speculation. Her particular talent is best suited to tasks requiring imagination and creativity as to her the unfamiliar presents a great challenge to be taken up.

Being intuitive, she is able to make rapid appraisals and assessments, allowing her sharp discerning mind to reach a conclusion without the need for too much conscious reasoning. High aspirations make it difficult for her to exercise total control over an extremely active imagination, but because her novel ideas often fall within a constructive framework they are able to play their part in her unique achievements. Instinctive feelings and idealistic dreams influence her far more than material and social considerations and there is no way that she will compromise her originality. A rebel against conformity for its own sake, she refuses to bow to any of the sacred cows of form and tradition, striving mightily to clear the ruts of convention.

Within her is a strong urge for continuous activity resulting from unstilled ambition and an unexplained dissatisfaction with that so far achieved. The constant craving for change and innovation is pushing her beyond the powers of even her considerable endurance and unless she succeeds in controlling her inner longings, albeit by continuous activity, then she may never be aware of what the discrepancy is between her considerable actual achievements and those to which she aspires in her dreams.

There is an exercising of intellectual independence and a refusal to court popularity and this can manifest itself in hostile displays towards the more restricting demands of the day. Pugnacious and headstrong, she can, when she deems it necessary, be quarrelsome and litigious, and this mixture makes her difficult to live with. Nevertheless, she is a protector of the weak and rarely if ever does an appeal to her magnanimity go unanswered.

Sudden enthusiasms are harnessed and just as quickly allowed to subside, but in spite of this she is a person of great conviction with a willingness to fight for her beliefs; one of which is unshakeable, and that is the belief in herself. Since she holds strong convictions she can in turn convince others. These are the qualities required for leadership.

Considerable extroversion means that she has many friends but nearly all of them are kept at a rather superficial level. If you were at a party with Jean Rook you would soon become aware of her preference for spending a small amount of time with as many people as possible rather than monopolizing one person all evening. This is primarily due to her need for regular stimulation. Expansiveness is at the core of her social relationships; she blossoms forth when with others and tends to wither when alone for any length of time. She thrives on risk and excitement and really comes to life when going flat-out in pursuit of a new project. Routine desk work is anathema to her as she loves to keep on the move. Idealistic, with a deep longing to make something of her dreams, there is an eagerness to develop opportunities and to grasp whatever is offered in the way of a fresh challenge.

Living very much through her senses, she is well able to understand the natural order of things and this allows her instinctively to combine events and happenings in her individual and distinctive style. There is a justified pride in her achievements and a flamboyant demand for attention indicating a subconscious desire for recognition. She is also concerned with, and alert to, the impact of her message upon others and its effect upon her prestige. This, however, is in conflict with her attitude of 'work before friendship' and 'satisfaction of a job well done', before rest and relaxation. These attitudes are not totally inflexible, though, as she is able to adjust her stance and change her mind as and when she is sufficiently impressed with another person's opinions and suggestions. If she was unable to experience these temporary uncertainties, with their resulting mobility and modifications of her views, then she would be unable to progress any further.

These temporary uncertainties also enable her to fit her career to her family responsibilities, which is fortunate as she considers her family to be her most important possession and a major stabilizing force in her otherwise tumultuous life. Her greatest fear is that she should lose their approval of what she has achieved, for, without their support, success would indeed be hollow. Emotional scenes are not uncommon in her life due to the difficulty she has in controlling her strong feelings and impulses, but they should never be taken too seriously as shortly after, all is forgotten. Not only is she incapable of holding a grudge for long but she finds it difficult to understand those who do.

Occasionally she will look on the black side and let pessimism act as a deterrent to the processing of new ideas, but, in general, Jean Rook has come to terms with herself in relation to the reality of what she is and what she does, and there is a resultant regulation of her life to what can only be described as . . . a most useful purpose.

'A very good analysis of my entire character' — Jean Rook

Contrast

Contrasting – or conflicting – emotions and attitudes are usually represented by writing that is overlarge and/or by conflicting slopes to the writing strokes. Whatever the other qualities featured in the writing, it is these two that expose any opposing pulls within the personality.

Oliver Reed

Dear Derek.
    Would be pleased to know
if you think I'm as "bonkers"
as "I think I am." *Oliver Reed*.

HANDWRITING HIGHLIGHTS

Many letters not connected to their neighbour point to Oliver Reed being highly intuitive, and the legible script indicates his desire to be understood. Bars crossing high on the letter 't' as well as strong strokes in the upper zone demonstrate that he is given to much intellectual speculation towards future projects. The writing is quite rigid and this shows that he is a worrier who likes to have as much control as possible over his environment. Uneven pressure in this writing relates to loss of emotional control and outbursts of anger. The flamboyance of the signature reveals this characteristic in his personality. Hooks at the beginning and end of many strokes certainly state that here is a man with considerable nervous energy and tenacity of purpose. The writing shows both enthusiasm and inertia so that it is difficult for him to project his vision as his moods interrupt his thought processes. To see this clearly all that is necessary is to take into account the large, apparently strong writing and then set this off against weaknesses such as the left tendencies in all three zones.

In general, the letters are placed close together, which shows quite clearly that he is not an easygoing man and that he is quite capable of being needlessly unco-operative. His writing is larger than life and so is he.

PORTRAIT

Oliver Reed is an intuitive man, able to assess a situation without the need for much reasoning. There is a desire to be understood, as he is a sincere and transparent charac-ter who does not think it necessary to conceal traits within himself or to distort facts. He does, however, shrink from being seen through and tends to conceal his intentions, pretending to be simple and slow in his reactions while all the time he has a brain which works alertly. He is a good speaker and stylist, efficient in the spheres of practi-cal life.

Driven by a deep longing to make something of his dreams, he fully explores all areas of his life and exercises his agile mind with intellectual speculation. This can lead to some fantasizing as he has difficulty in controlling his emotions and his fertile imagination, so it is not surprising that there is a certain lack of objectivity, and an inabil-ity to be subordinate, a lack of modesty and tact and some neglect of reality. Countering this, there is a justifi-able pride in his achievements, a generosity bordering on the extravagant, self-reliance and broadmindedness, all of which give him the confidence to pursue his aims with tenacity.

He is rather cautious and is also a worrier who likes to establish as much control over his environment as possible, and whilst his moods are fairly even and predictable he can show a strong outburst of temper when his control snaps. He tends to dislike 'situations' where things can get out of hand as he has difficulty in displaying his inner feelings. If the occasion demands, though, he can put on an outer show of friendliness and give the impression that he is revealing his real self even though it is highly unlikely that he would do so. He can be needlessly uncooperative and will obstinately concentrate upon a subject long after the need has gone, thus wasting a lot of his nervous energy. He resents restraint because he needs freedom of thought and action in his everyday life, but his cool aversion to restriction is more than compensated for by his warm enthusiasm for those matters in which he is really interested — whether in work or leisure they will be met by lively energy.

There is often a flamboyant demand for attention from a mind which is very much occupied with the effects of his message and whether it has been understood, and this can upset the balance of his judgement and the reliability of his efforts. He tries to overcome obstacles by the force of his personality, and if he fails he simply does not admit the fact, being satisfied with the illusion of success. He is able to do this because his standards possess no objective accuracy and he only accepts reality in so far as it conforms to his subjective ideals. This is a useful trait as it enables him to carry out projects which a person with a more objective sense of reality would give up as hopeless. He has a small number of real friends who he values highly and he is prepared to work hard to maintain these relationships. If the atmosphere is sufficiently relaxed then he will be too.

He does tend to be rather changeable and to live for the moment. It is difficult for him to project his vision as his moods and whims interrupt his thinking and he appears to be always seeking new interests in a life which seems to lack a definite pattern.

His constant desire to escape from the demands made by his inner self results in continuous activity without pause for reflection, which ultimately produces little that is finished or concrete. He seeks compensation for the lack of a definite goal, and when even momentarily inactive becomes bored, which can lead him into groups where activity takes the form of pursuit of self-indulgent and often hollow pleasures.

Oliver Reed is, like his handwriting, larger then life, and like any bright light he burns fiercely and clears away the shadows from those around him.

'Yes! Good! How kind!' — Oliver Reed

Jimmy Greaves

Look to This day for it
is life.
Yesterday is but a dream
Tomorrow only a vision
Today well spent makes
every yesterday a dream
of happiness, and every
tomorrow a vision of hope!

Left Hand.

Jimmy Greaves

HANDWRITING HIGHLIGHTS

Within this script there are many disconnected letters and this feature of handwriting strongly points to the writer's ability to solve problems by intuition rather than through reason and logic. Capital letters are used in the middle of words where one would normally find lower case, and when combined with the long lower loops to letters such as 'g' and 'y', this feature tells us of his liking for physical action. The writing shows a mixture of strength and weakness, aggression and passivity, and these opposing features account for much of the conflict that is so obviously present. A slight left slant to the writing is quite normal for left-handed people, and yet here we have a slant to the right that is quite pronounced in parts. It is therefore safe to assume that the slant to the right is excessive and indicates his reliance upon others and his need for contact with them.

Whilst the surname – which represents the public side – is just about decipherable, the christian name is most certainly not, and this is a classic illustration of a man who likes to keep his private life just that — private.

PORTRAIT

Leaping out at you from the handwriting of Jimmy Greaves is his intuitiveness, his ability to make quick appraisals and assessments just prior to reaching a conclusion, all achieved without the need for a lot of reasoning beforehand. He can at times give the impression that he is not 'with it' but the reality is that his sharp mind is grasping the essentials of whatever is happening so that his intelligence can make good use of the findings. He strives, but is not always successful, to achieve a harmony of the mind by trying to realize only those things which fall within his scope and not go beyond himself, but there is an element of unrest in the make-up, a lack of coherency with a tendency to soar to spiritual heights before plunging to instinctual depths. The impulses are strong and there is a dissatisfaction with that so far achieved as well as from unfulfilled ambition. Also strong within him is a desire for change and innovation and this can urge him on to go beyond his natural limitations. If he succeeds in satisfying his ambitions by continual activity he may remain unaware of the gulf between his actual achievements and those he is dreaming about. If, however, he fails to find this outlet then the result will be extreme dissatisfaction, black moods and nagging despair. Continuous activity could also lead to him overtaxing his energy — a familiar by-product of those whose enthusiasm carries them beyond their natural capacity.

He has the ability for clear expression and is a good speaker and stylist, and there is little ambiguity in what he says. Anxiety and emotional pressure, however, tend to influence him too intensely so that there are times when he loses his objectivity. Talkative and rather tense, it is the activity of his imagination which drives him to attain his objectives and as a result he is a man who prefers to be always on the move, becoming restless when confined behind a desk. Equally apparent is his search for perfection and the deep longing to make something of his dreams, and he can devise a course of action to help him achieve these aims with a mind completely unfettered by material considerations. These are the times when he is impractical and rather vulnerable.

The inherent excitability of the personality is instinctive and is brought about by past experiences which, whilst being rejected by him, nevertheless still tend to threaten. He can find himself both elated and despondent in turn, and it can take very little to bring about the change; nevertheless there is a good degree of determination and purpose as he has constructed an effective defence against his temperamental impressionability. He is

a vital person who is fond of people although he does not
like being obligated to or indeed ordered about by anyone.
The will is strong and he is ready to fight for what he
believes is right and there is in his make-up an exacting
persistence which enables him to forge ahead in whatever he undertakes and in spite of any opposition. There
are, in varying degrees, aggressiveness, assertiveness and
obstinacy, and the tongue can be sharp. So, from all this,
you can see that there is inner turmoil, for the emotions are
as quick-changing as the hand that guides the pen. When
conflict does arise between the emotions and the intellect,
however, then it is the intellect that usually wins, for it
manages to sit in judgement on the feelings and control
them for a while.

There are signs of self-interest present in the writing,
along with impatience and a lack of concentration, but
in his dealings with others he will use his shrewd mind
and exercise tact and diplomacy at the right time so
that these features do not interfere with the successful
outcome of his aims. He has a strong desire to express
himself and to communicate, and with his inclination
towards extroversion and need for contact with others
he enjoys an interesting social life — with himself usually
the centre of attention. He moves under emotional tension and his impetus is not checked by excessive control so that there is a daring about him and a readiness
to come out into the open unreservedly and reveal his
thoughts. Rather than the abstract, he tends to deal in
matters concrete in an intuitive and imaginative way and
is more compelled by impulse than guided by considered
reasoning. In spite of outward appearances there is some
lack of inner assuredness, and on occasion he seeks and
needs a conflict haven. He is natural and unconstrained,
and he lives and relies on his senses; in every way he is a
human being near to life and nature.

This creative individual, full of imaginative ideas, is liable to jump to conclusions and make hasty decisions on

the strength of instinct and intuition. For those who are cautious, this is not the way; but for true achievers such as Jimmy Greaves, it is the only way.

'I found the analysis very interesting' — Jimmy Greaves

David Hamilton

Dear Derek,

Many thanks for your letter.
My handwriting has always been atrocious —
so make of it what you will!
As you may gather, I am right handed.
I look forward — with some trepidation — to reviewing

from you.

Best wishes,

David Hamilton

HANDWRITING HIGHLIGHTS

David Hamilton is the victim of his emotions as is clearly shown in his handwriting by the conflicting slants to his letters and the uneven pressure pattern throughout. When the capital letter 'I' is placed close to the following letter and yet distanced from the preceding one it clearly indicates that the person concerned functions better when with others and should not spend too much time alone. The bars that cross the letter 't' are weak and do not always go through the stem and this means that he is a person who is easily influenced. The writing in the signature is the same as the rest of the script, so we have here a man who is without pretension, and in public or private he will behave the same.

PORTRAIT

David Hamilton is a pleasant and rather conventional person who is fairly easygoing and not too well disciplined. He behaves quite naturally and there is no wish to assume a behaviour in private which would reflect a different face to that which he shows to his public. He can work well without constant attention as he is well able to motivate himself. He is somewhat self-effacing and modest, and does not actively seek acclaim, which means that he is able to accept constructive criticism from those he considers able to guide him. There is a sensitive side to his nature, and feelings of uncertainty have on occasion prevented him from making the most of an opportunity that has been presented.

He has adapted to the world and the demands that it has made on him, but the adaptation does not spring from his inner being; rather it is a sham adaptation into which he has forced himself through necessity. He does not find it easy to express his deepest feelings although he displays initiative and effectiveness in his outward expression. Some difficulties are experienced with people, because they rarely live up to his preconceived image of what they should be. Yet he is quite warm-hearted and tends therefore to be unduly influenced by others. Whilst he is undoubtedly emotional he can nevertheless exercise good control over his feelings, and when he has to make a decision his head is quite capable of ruling his heart.

Rather a conventional man, he has developed habits of obedience to prescribed routine and he prefers to operate within this framework; an instinctive desire to strike out on his own and make something of his dreams is prohibited by an unexplained reluctance.

There are a number of other conflicting impulses; for instance, there is his wish to express himself more and to experiment in new and untried areas which is countered by his desire to nurture and protect that which he has. Realism can also give way to flights of fancy, and ambition to complacency. He can vary between moments of withdrawn solitude and periods of excited sociability. This conflicting outlook is caused by a breakdown in the application of self-discipline, and at such times he is more strongly compelled by his emotions than he is guided by reasoning.

His imagination is unconsciously and instinctively active so that in addition to creative planning there is some fanciful and wishful thinking. Many ideas flow through his mind, but he cannot always progress through them logically, step by step. His tendency is to keep rolling along avoiding friction, and when necessary he can exercise tact and diplomacy to achieve this. However well he might adjust, there are still unexpressed longings which disturb him and these give rise to a restless dissatisfaction with his efforts so far. As a result, activity is somewhat fitful and unsustained and he can become irritable and find it difficult to direct his energies in a positive way. Busy all the time, he seems to lack a singleness of purpose, but he is versatile and capable of doing many things well. He sometimes lacks the perseverance to finish what he starts and it is not easy for him to maintain an interest in a subject over an extended period.

He functions better when in company and becomes uneasy on his own, but his wish to be independent enables him to control the uneasiness and make positive use of time spent alone.

He has a practical outlook on life and is prudent in his personal affairs, with a methodical way of handling finance. He is not particularly philosophical and tends to act as his instincts dictate, seeking a degree of satisfaction in life by indulging his physical appetites.

There is a restlessness and a conflict between the emotions and the mind, but because he is not particularly goal-minded he can become very enthusiastic over a new idea or situation while he is planning what to do; yet by the time he is ready to take action the novelty has worn off, his enthusiasm has waned and he has turned to something else. He can be whimsical, changeable and often self-indulgent, and this makes it difficult for him to project his vision as his moods interrupt his thinking. He seems always to be seeking new interests, and there is a continuous desire to escape from the demands made by his inner self. The problem here is that to concentrate on one thing at a time might bring him into contact with those facts about his life that he does not wish to face, so he takes refuge in continuous activity without pause for reflection, and his actions produce little that is really concrete or conclusive.

David Hamilton is not always an easy man to understand, but there is a vitality about him which ensures that while in his company you are never bored.

'I would say the profile is quite accurate' — David Hamilton

Terry Scott

I suppose we all try
to write better when under
examination, However I am
not in the least doing so

yours

Terry Scott

Right Handed

HANDWRITING HIGHLIGHTS

Here is a personality mixture of oversensitiveness and self-
assurance, as shown by the pressure variation throughout
the handwriting. This conflict has beset him with doubts

about his ability and in turn has prevented him from making the most of past opportunities. This is also indicated by the unrhythmic writing, the uneven baseline and the uneven height of the middle zone letters. He is pushed along by his impulses rather than guided by reasoned thought, which in his writing is indicated by narrow word spacing. His rich but somewhat out-of-balance personality is revealed by the illegible handwriting that contains many original letter forms, while a tendency to conceal himself from others is shown by the way in which he overstrokes many letters. The fluctuating width of the writing reflects his mercurial emotions, and his moodiness and impulsiveness are represented by the erratic nature of the script in general. If you examine the writing carefully you will see that there is an underlying strength in the way the letters are formed and connected, there are no weak or hesitant strokes, and this is the feature that shows there is much left for him to give.

PORTRAIT

Terry Scott has a mind that is full of curiosity and not hidebound by the normal conventions, and this has led to him making some unique achievements throughout his life to date. Imagination as well as external impressions influence him greatly, and his feelings and impulses are not easily controlled and kept in check — he is in fact a rather hasty and unpredictable man and there is an underlying irrationality in his make-up which makes him observe life with some inconsistency. Moody and excitable, he is restless and dissatisfied with what he has accomplished so far. It is difficult for him to decide exactly what it is he really wants from life as his aims are ever changing, and with his fluctuating emotionality he is pulled between a desire to try something new and the need to follow the more protected paths of the known. He is a sensitive person who suffers doubts about his capabilities, and this has in the past prevented him from making the most of his opportunities.

He is more often propelled by his feelings than guided by his intellect and this introduces a restlessness into his persona and creates an atmosphere whereby his energies fail to find sufficient outlet.

He can be assertive and over-opinionated and will display a lack of tolerance towards anyone who he believes is interfering in his affairs.

There is some artificiality, and on occasion he can be seen behaving in a rather elaborately contrived way; this is merely for outward display — not the genuine expression of the inner man, but a defence against his self-consciousness. By the same token he has adapted himself to the world and the demands it makes upon him, suppressing his real needs, desires and feelings in favour of those required for his occupation.

There is a reserve, and a great reluctance to show his inner feelings, and as a result he hides away the real Terry Scott from all but his closest associates. He is very self-involved and rather unsure of himself, which traits have denied him the opportunity of developing his skills as fully as he would have wished.

The personality of Terry Scott is rich in talent, highly original and just a touch off-key. As a result he is not always willing to adapt himself to his circumstances or to society in general, and this creates conflict and stress within his psyche.

He is not too interested in the social demands of the day and therefore is not particularly considerate towards the needs of others. A mixture of feeling and intuition makes him unpredictable, and it is when this unpredictability is combined with his talent that he gives of his best. Although the handwriting is poorly laid out, it has a dominantly strong appearance, which clearly shows that in spite of his conflicts there remains great potential.

'Terry says it is frighteningly accurate and, knowing him as well as I do, I agree with that' — Guy Lane, Personal Manager

Denis Norden, CBE

Dear Mr Holmes,

Thank you for your letter. Beyond passing on the information that I am right-handed, I can't honestly think of three or four lines of waffle for you to analyse.

Don't make it ~~too~~ startling will you.

Yours sincerely,

Denis Nod—

HANDWRITING HIGHLIGHTS

Beneath the laid-back exterior of Denis Norden there lurks an excitable temperament as evidenced by the conflicting slants of the letter strokes. The complete absence of starting, or lead-in, strokes to the first letter of the words clearly demonstrates that he wastes little time on matters which he considers unimportant. Many of the letters such as 'm' or 'n' are formed in an angular fashion which shows that he is able to concentrate on his work even under the most trying of conditions. The lines of writing slope upwards and additionally they are serpentine, or wavy. This means that he is versatile and has a pleasant, hopeful outlook on life. He presses his pen heavily on the paper, so there is good energy potential, and the strokes are firm, which points to the strong will and the ability to concentrate. The varying lengths of the bars that cross the 't's indicate that he has not only the ability to work for today but also the talent for planning well ahead. Small hooks at the beginning and end of many strokes are a sure sign that he is a tense and talkative individual who finds it difficult to relax.

PORTRAIT

A speculative mind; a desire to be understood; consideration for the feelings of others, and sincerity — all these combine to make only part of the many-sided personality of Denis Norden. Active imagination fires his never-resting mind, driving him to attain his objectives, and this makes him tense, talkative and enthusiastic. His homogenous mixture of imagination and intelligence enables him first to visualize an idea and then to make the vision take on practical form. He likes to get down to matters quickly, wasting little time on things he considers unimportant, and he prefers to concentrate upon the detail of a subject and study it profoundly.

The sharp ingenious mind rapidly grasps the essentials of an idea, and assessments of the potential are made quickly and intuitively rather than by lengthy reasoning and consideration. His emotional and intellectual sides are in balance, leaving the mind ever open to new impressions and further knowledge.

The underlying nature is excitable and rather volatile but he has learned to exercise a strong control over his impressionability so that it is creatively directed. Sometimes the control is too strong, and this can give rise to an emotional silence, which can interfere with the free development of his genuine inner expression so that he might appear indifferent to values outside the rational and social world. Despite these occasional lapses, his sense of humour usually tempers his feelings so that he is able to see the funny side of even serious issues.

He makes no attempt to shirk or avoid responsibilities, preferring to overcome obstacles rather than adapt to them, and this gives him a strong purposeful use of his qualities in the fulfilment of his aims. He enjoys a pleasant, hopeful disposition, with the ability to concentrate on the task in hand even under difficult conditions, has an abundance of nervous energy, not being the type to stand still for long whether in speech or action, and will drive himself hard when pursuing an objective.

He is not a particularly good mixer as his interest in abstraction is greater than his interest in people, but he can put on a show of camaraderie when the occasion demands whilst still maintaining a degree of reluctance about revealing his true inner feelings. So, despite the appearance, you are unlikely to be seeing the real Denis Norden. He does like people, however, and he is well balanced and fairly uncomplicated in his approach to them; on the other hand, there is some difficulty encountered when adapting to the environment so that he tends towards nonconformity and a dislike of restriction and restraint. In the case of the latter it is because he needs freedom for both thought and action.

When he is truly interested in a subject he will really warm to it and give it his best shot — this ability to channel his creative talents lies at the heart of his success.

A summary of the personality of Denis Norden indicates a man who is witty and has a sense of humour; is well able to conceive ideas and take the initiative, carrying them through to a constructive conclusion. Rather unbending and even headstrong, he is reliable and thorough in whatever task he undertakes, and his supple mind will remain young, whatever his age. Sometimes he is subject to contradictory impulses — becoming extrovert and pulled toward the outside world on occasions, whilst at other times he shows reserve and distances himself from others.

He tends to be cautious and a bit of a worrier who likes to feel he has control over his working environment. His moods are fairly even and predictable, and there are good powers of concentration, making him good at work requiring attention to detail.

It is difficult for Denis Norden to relax and unwind and he is not the type to stand and stare, as his agile mind compels him into a state of on-going activity. When referring to this very individualistic person there is no more apt way of expressing the whole character than the saying 'You can't keep a good man down'.

'It's far too flattering, but use it anyway' — Denis Norden

Culture

The handwriting of a person of some culture must first and foremost be of a high form standard and pleasing to the eye. Another distinguishing feature is the use of the Greek style letters 'g' and 'e'.

Michael Aspel

Dear Mr. Holmes,

Thanks for your letter. I've always imagined my handwriting to be decorative and interesting, but most people just find it difficult to understand.

I hope I've written enough for your purposes. By the way, I'm right-handed. Good luck with the book.

Yrs. Michael Aspel

HANDWRITING HIGHLIGHTS

The easy fluent writing indicates the fluent thought processes, and the way in which he simplifies his letters can only come from an intelligent and creative mind. Culture is featured in the script by the Greek letters 'e' and 'g', many of which have the appearance of the figure eight. There are very few lead-in strokes to the first letter of words which points to his ability to get to the heart of a matter quite quickly without wasting time on preliminaries. The end strokes to the last letter of the majority of words are missing and this points to an abruptness in his dealings with others.

The signature, with both names linked, clearly signals that Michael Aspel is a distinctive and individual man, and the heavy underlining, followed by a full stop, shows that he likes to have the last word. Vitality and a fondness for people is shown by the medium pressure of the pen on the paper, and the upright nature of most strokes speaks volumes for his self-control.

PORTRAIT

The mind of Michael Aspel is restlessly active and full of curiosity about an unusually wide range of subjects and topics. He is efficient in his approach to work and the fluent thought processes clearly demonstrate that there is a high level of intelligence, which in turn means he is able to develop his practical ideas in a logical and rational manner. He has a good memory for detail and this trait is further enhanced by his ability to be attentive to whatever is the current task. Although always 'up and doing', he maintains an orderliness in his affairs, accomplished through the careful control he applies to his thought processes. There is an impressionable side to his nature, against which he has had to erect a defence to help keep his thoughts clear and reasoned. He can therefore appear clinical in his approach towards people, for he fears that getting too close too quickly could make him lose some of his objectivity. Nevertheless, beneath it all he is a friendly person, socially helpful and comparatively free from sentimentality and conciliatoriness. Well-adjusted, impartial and with a generous topping of realism, he has a direct approach to situations requiring his attention as he does not wish to waste time on non-essentials. He is able to concentrate on what he is doing even when conditions are unfavourable, as he is mainly preoccupied with the here-and-now and only rarely does he daydream. The fact is, he is a bit of a fatalist, and takes things just as they come.

He has an overwhelming desire to express himself in his own particular style and will not compromise on this issue. Rather surprisingly he does not court popularity for its own sake and is not inclined to adapt himself too readily to his surroundings; neither is he too concerned with the social demands that are made upon him. Similarly, although he is fairly easygoing, he is not a particularly considerate person when he is working, and at those times he can be unpredictable and difficult to understand.

There are distinct signs of a fluctuating emotionality in the sample of handwriting that indicate that he possesses a strong sense of humour and the ability to laugh. It also indicates that while he is in control of his feelings, for much of the time he can, when frustrated, blow his top in no uncertain manner.

It is difficult to separate his private from his public life as he behaves much the same in either, and lives just as easily in each. Also indicated is what can only be described as a mischievous side to his character. This can manifest itself in a number of ways, the way, for instance, in which he takes a special delight in appearing vague and obscure; this, however, is just another part of the personality of this distinctive and individual man and should not be taken to mean any more than that.

He has come to know himself and has thereby found a measure of security in his life. By being neither too pushy nor too retiring, Michael Aspel certainly makes it look easy, but that which enables him to do this is the way in which he projects his persona in a quietly confident manner. The way is unique to the man and it is a way that just cannot be ignored.

'I think you've produced a set of perceptive observations' — Michael Aspel

Sir Harry Secombe, CBE

Dear DERK

I hope these few lines will give you some clues to my character — it's not the best handwriting in the world but it's all I've got! Any chemist will translate it for you.

Sincerely

Harry Secombe

HANDWRITING HIGHLIGHTS

He wants to be understood and this is clearly shown by the legibility of his writing, which also means that he is sincere and with a character that is transparent and without falsehood. Aestheticism is indicated by the Greek letter 'e' as well as the finely balanced capitals. The flamboyant signature tells you that he is fond of good living, although the narrow left margin shows his caution. There are sufficient hard-to-read letters for us to know that he likes to do his own thing and go his own way. Strong bars crossing the 't's state clearly that he is also not easily swayed by the views of others, which stability can also be seen in the straight lines of writing.

If you examine the letters 'm' 'n' and 'h' you will see that they are constructed from soft, rather wavy, lines called garlands and this is a sure sign of a kind and obliging nature. Nevertheless there are some angles present and these inject a firmness into the personality that gives it balance.

PORTRAIT

Notwithstanding the fact that Sir Harry Secombe is both independent and self-reliant he is also a charming and obliging person. His character sincere, transparent and completely without falsehood and ambiguity, he is anxious that people should understand him. Being warm-hearted and sensitive means that, although he is naturally drawn towards the outside world, there is also a reserve, a questioning, a recognition that sometimes he would like a more 'normal' lifestyle; but when such thoughts intrude, his self-control is able to overcome the impressionability. He approaches everything he does with concentration and diligence so that he is able to pursue his aims with a steadiness and regularity; rarely if ever is he carried away by impulse.

His aesthetic and artistic interests are reflected by his abilities, a successful formula which fully justifies his self-esteem and pride in achievement.

The personality is well-integrated and in tune with the realities of everyday life, although there is a side to his character that tends to procrastinate, to delay action until the last moment.

He has a mature approach to most things but does not always exercise the same control towards himself: an example of this would be his fondness for attractive clothes, good living and a desire for an interesting social life. His inclination towards extroversion means that he can work at a project if he has to, but he is a doer rather than one who is inclined towards meditation.

His character is upright and, perhaps rather surprisingly, a little stiff and inflexible; this does mean, though, that he is reliable and thorough in whatever he undertakes — with his go and energy, therefore, he not only aspires to the more lofty goals, he achieves them as well.

He is essentially a social being, aware of the needs of others and always prepared to lend a helping hand, and this instinctive sympathy and tolerant good nature means that he has many friends. He is confident in his relations with others and can strike up an acquaintance with a stranger at the drop of a hat and is not put off if the initial response is not forthcoming. He will speak out forthrightly in defence of his principles, but such is his need to express his views that he will become irritated if he thinks that they are not being taken seriously enough.

He lives a useful, well-regulated life, which he finds fulfilling, and his steadfastness enables him to deal effectively with changing circumstances. Morally he can clearly distinguish between that which is right and that which is wrong, and there is no way that he will blur his conscious distinction. There is no pretension in his make-up, and he is modest and unassuming in both his public and private life; and as he is not dependent upon public acclaim for his self-esteem there is no need to sacrifice any part of either existence. Sir Harry Secombe still retains sufficient ambition to satisfy his need for achievement and he still tends to regard obstacles as challenges rather than difficulties. From all that I have learned through the analysis of his handwriting, he does appear to have the rare distinction of being the same person both privately and publicly. What you see is what he is, genuine and unaffected.

'Delighted with what you have had to say about me' — Sir Harry Secombe

Thora Hird, OBE

Dear Mr Holmes,

Thank you most kindly for your letter — I hope this little note will provide you with sufficient words for you to work on.

Meanwhile, take care and God bless you,

Thora Hird

HANDWRITING HIGHLIGHTS

This is a very legible script with most, if not all, letters and words easily recognizable either in or out of context, which clearly indicates the writer's inherent sincerity. There is much use of the Greek 'e', which is representative of culture, and the generally well proportioned and aesthetically stylized letters certainly demonstrate her love of beauty in all its forms. There are many spire strokes which have their beginnings high above the

base line of the writing — more clearly than any other factor these reveal her spirituality. Her sense of achievement
is shown by the good layout, and the excellently spaced
words and lines speak strongly of her orderly approach to
life. All the bars crossing the letter 't' are wavy, and this
most strongly indicates her fun-loving nature and ability
to laugh. The signature, which is identical to the general
writing, displays her naturalness; her constancy could not
be more clearly stated than by the underlinings of certain
parts of the writing: in each case the design is the same
and it is followed by a full stop, revealing that her word
does tend to be final, although with her kindly approach
to people she is certainly not tyrannical.

PORTRAIT

Thora Hird is a person of aesthetic and cultural refinement
with a passion for beauty in all its forms. Moreover, she
is idealistic and with a spirituality that gives her a deep
understanding of the poetic qualities of life. She is a
sensitive, sincere and kindly person whose words are
as unambiguous as her character is transparent, whose
personality is well-integrated and harmonious, and who
has a real talent for fluently expressing her every thought.
Efficiency in the sphere of practical life gives her a positive and genuine outlook, and sensitivity combines with
this to provide a capacity for pondering the whys and
wherefores of life.

'A place for everything and everything in its place' describes another side of her character as the orderly mind
displays a strong organizing flair. Her outlook is independent, giving her a calm and reliable approach to matters so
that she is able to remain cool when others panic. There is
also the capacity for concentrated and disciplined work,
which enables her to pursue whatever is her current task
both steadily and regularly.

She can at times be outspoken, even over-opinionated, and will defend her beliefs forthrightly; nevertheless, she understands that the line between frankness and rudeness is easily crossed, and so she will exercise tact and restraint at the right time, going just so far with her point of view, then pausing to take stock of the situation before pursuing it farther.

There are some feelings of uncertainty, some looking inwards and to the past, and some regrets that things which should have been done have been left undone. There are still some unfulfilled ambitions which she would like to satisfy but not at the cost of her happiness and contentment.

Although she is not given to great displays of emotion, she is a warm person with a sense of humour and a love of fun. There is a real fondness for people, and she is neither pushy nor retiring in her approach to them. With her good nature and willingness to help others, and adaptability, she enjoys a natural relationship with those around her as well as with the world at large, and she experiences no difficulty in making contact socially. She lives a full life to useful purpose, and in so doing has gained a sense of achievement and satisfaction.

Thora Hird has gained fame and recognition whilst still retaining the inherent kindliness of her nature. This is indeed a rare combination and one that is achieved by very few whose life is spent mainly in the glare of the spotlight.

'I really enjoyed your remarkable personality profile of my mother' — Janette Scott

Sir John Mills, CBE

Dear Mr Holmes,
Here are
the few lines you require.
May I take this opportunity
to wish you a very happy
New Year.
Yours,

John Mills.

HANDWRITING HIGHLIGHTS

The middle zone is reasonably balanced but there are some negative features, and this negativity indicates that in spite of any adjustments that might have been made, he is still frequently disturbed by longings that are difficult to identify. The letters slope to the right, which shows that he is interested in the world and what is happening there.

Medium width of letters reflect self-possession and control of the feelings, but the fluctuating width of the space between the letters reveals that he varies between intolerance and friendliness. Pressure on horizontal strokes certainly indicates aggression within the personality, and pressure on the last letter of many words points to his need to have the last word. Capital letters are simply formed, well-proportioned and graceful — qualities which, in writing, are indicative of artistic interests and ability, good taste, and a sense of proportion within the character of the writer. Inner harmony is shown by the good rhythm of the writing, and control of the feelings is again indicated by the general regularity of the script. We have, in the christian name and surname being written as one word, a very strong indication that the writing is that of a distinctive and individual person.

PORTRAIT

Sir John Mills combines culture, good taste and intellectuality with artistic sensitivity, which allows him to arrange his life aesthetically. His mind is rich in ideas and genuinely versatile so that he has the facility in his art for infinite variation. The imagination is in balance, with the intellect enabling him to put his thoughts to practical use. He is compelled towards the outside world and has an abiding interest in all that is taking place there, and therefore enjoys lively debate and argument. His mind is so active that he will indulge in argument for its own sake if no suitable outlet can be found for his thoughts, although there is a great flexibility, indicating that he is well able to modify his stance and change his opinions as and when he is sufficiently impressed with the views of others.

His outlook on life can be somewhat inconsistent — as one day he will examine things in great detail, whilst on other occasions he might well take a broader view. He has strong opinions and can be outspoken when occasion demands, and certain occurrences such as unnecessary delays can move him from a general air of calmness to impatient intolerance. In spite of occasional and well-calculated outbursts, his words are tempered with tact and restraint although an inherent impulsiveness does lead him sometimes to do what he must as soon possible even if later he has cause to regret his action.

He possesses a generous nature which is fortunately guided by his mature personality so that he is not influenced unduly by the demands of others. Within him there are unexpressed yearnings for things he still wishes to accomplish as well as for things that have long since gone.

There is a strong desire to enjoy an interesting social life built around those he finds stimulating; this wish for companionship, however, is countered by an inner reserve and independence, giving him the ability to function quite well when by himself.

The mind is strong and disciplined and his instincts can be trusted. He is able to speak out forthrightly in defence of his beliefs, and he has complete confidence in his ability to cope with the daily challenges of life. It is hard to shake his confidence and as a result he is prepared to take chances in the pursuit of that which gives him satisfaction.

There is a modesty and a moderation about him which springs from his able mind, which not only imparts contentment and inner harmony to him, but also means that he can, in turn, impart these qualities to those with whom he comes into contact. He is a distinctive and individual man who has a genuine pride in his achievements, and both his public and private lives are important to him in equal measure. Certainly, he has come to terms with himself and his life in relation to their reality and has found great satisfaction. The handwriting shows quite clearly that he has enjoyed the ride aboard the vehicle of his chosen profession, and as a result he is unlikely ever to step off completely.

'An enlightening analysis which I thoroughly enjoyed reading' — Sir John Mills

Durability

Narrow spacing and strong connecting strokes between letters, sharp angles that appear unexpectedly, heavy pressure in the horizontal as well as the vertical strokes and long swing underlengths are all indicators of a strong and durable character.

Geoff Capes

Dear Derek,

Many thanks for your letter I find your request quite interesting. It would be quite funny for another person to tell me who I am and what I should be. in life other than what I am.

Regards

Geoff Capes

P.S. dont tell me I'm a nut I already know!!

HANDWRITING HIGHLIGHTS

The tension of the strokes that link the letters together is very strong, and this points to great strength of will, while the upright nature of the writing in general depicts the control that he applies to feelings and impulses. Sincerity, and honesty of purpose and intent, are shown by the legibility of the script. The strong capital letter 'I' show that there is good self-esteem and self-confidence, and the regular size of the middle zone letters such as 'a' 'o' and 'r' also reveals his emotional stability. The flamboyant side of him is exposed by the over-decorated capitals. In the construction of numerous letters he uses angles, wavy lines and arches or arcades and this points to Geoff Capes being a friendly, adaptable person, with more than just a hint of firmness in his make-up.

PORTRAIT

The life and work of Geoff Capes are strongly influenced by the strength of his will, and to those matters that he considers important he is invariable in his approach. Also emerging from the handwriting is the disciplined reliability, the powers of endurance, and the attributes of persistence, energy and thoroughness. The combination of these factors gives him his singleness of purpose, and it is this particular quality, possibly above all others, that has enabled him to achieve so much.

He is always enthusiastic when pursuing a chosen goal and at such times he can become irritated by, and impatient with, the more mundane sides of a project. He likes to keep on the move, and if he is kept in one place for too long he feels restricted and becomes restless and uneasy. There is an unyielding quality about him, and he does not allow outside influences to deter him from his chosen path.

He is a straightforward man whose life is fairly well regulated, which he likes as it gives him a feeling of security. He has a serious side to his nature and is both sincere and honest in his efforts, and there is a desire for orthodoxy. Rather conservative in his approach, he treats new ideas with caution and he is not given to displaying his emotions easily. If his pride is hurt he will bottle up his feelings and put on a brave face — this can make him somewhat moody, although the moods never last for long. There is a part of himself which he rarely if ever reveals, and this contains feelings of uncertainty and insecurity which he keeps hidden. The effect they have on his disposition is to make it rather changeable, although not disturbingly so, and they can also make him over-careful, so that he does not always realize what is and what is not essential. This in turn can lead to indecisiveness, although not to procrastination. It could also account for the impulsiveness which leads to him saying things which, in his more thoughtful periods, he might wish he had kept to himself.

Generally, the thinking is rational and consistent, with only the occasional flights of fancy, and normally this helpful person goes quietly about his business, acting in a sympathetic and understanding manner. There are, however, some contradictory impulses: for example, he is a moderate man, who can on occasion be pretentious, proud and arrogant — and why not, as there appears to be sufficient justification for these feelings? He is freedom-loving, and there is a flamboyant, almost theatrical, side to his nature which enables him to take the initiative and attract attention to himself. This exuberance is mainly displayed to gain more space to accommodate his need for self-expression. He knows what is right and what is wrong, and with his marked ethical tendencies there is no way that he will compromise his integrity. He manages to balance the demands made upon him both publicly and privately in a way that avoids bringing them into conflict with each other. It is, therefore, hardly surprising that Geoff Capes holds the title of the 'World's Strongest Man' as he possesses a character that is as strong as his physique, and that is indeed a formidable combination.

'I find the assessment most interesting' — Geoff Capes

Gordon Honeycombe

It now seems certain that Mrs Thatcher will refuse to allow her Press Secretary, Bernard Ingham, and her senior Private Secretary, Charles Powell, to go before the committee next week.
The rebuff is likely to provoke a bitter row in the Commons, with MPs from all parties protesting at the snub.

Gordon Honeycombe —

right-handed

HANDWRITING HIGHLIGHTS

The signature is identical in every respect to the rest of the handwriting, and from this we can safely assume that Gordon Honeycombe is natural and unpretentious in his behaviour. The letters are joined together with determined strokes, revealing a strong sense of purpose, and the even height of the middle zone letters speaks of self-confidence and self-assurance. The capital letters 'I' point to his businesslike approach with their top and bottom horizontal strokes. The writing overall tends towards rigidity, and this indicates the need to control his working surroundings as well as the desire to keep his emotions and feelings in check. The slight slope to the right of many strokes points to his wish to surge forward and rid himself of restraint, but the upright strokes which appear throughout tell quite clearly that he is unable to allow this. Again we have the head ruling the heart, which is just another way of saying that there is good self-discipline.

PORTRAIT

The handwriting of Gordon Honeycombe clearly shows that he has a penetrating insight into human activities and relationships. He is a clear and purposeful thinker, well able to make himself understood by others, and this is particularly important to a man whose main desire is that he should be able to express his individuality and develop a style all of his own.

His mind is sufficiently well balanced between the demands of the ego in everyday life, and a consideration for the reality of objects and other people. His feet are firmly planted on the ground and there are few, if any, pretensions. There is a conflict between the need to express himself and the need to protect his singularity and this discrepancy causes him to pause before taking even a calculated risk regarding his career progression. The anxiety arising from this indecision can on occasion influence him too intently, causing under certain circumstances a lack of objectivity, but he usually gives the appearance of being cool and matter-of-fact in his approach to difficulties.

He is interested in the world about him, but tends to view its happenings rather reflectively, discovering true expression only in his work and through that finding the outlet to develop and satisfy his emotional needs. His way of thinking is consistent and rational and gives him a strong sense of purpose, enabling him to make good progress with whatever is currently occupying his energies.

His life and work are powerfully influenced by willpower and this gives him the inner strength and harmony to make the resultant viewpoints and outlook both well balanced and mature. His strength of will also means that once he has made up his mind to accomplish something he will concentrate on it to the exclusion of all else. Dogged and determined, he advances on his chosen goal making no attempt to shirk any difficulties with which he might be confronted, and at such times you would find him hard, awkward and not at all easygoing.

Rather than emphatic gestures, he is given more to understatement and exercises prudence in his personal affairs. He is a very genuine person, reserved yet self-confident, seldom experiencing any real difficulty in making social contact, and whilst his circle of real friends is small he works very hard at developing and maintaining the relationships. There is abundant nervous energy, which makes it difficult for him to slow down and relax and he is always on the go and rarely able to remain idle for long.

To recap then: Gordon Honeycombe has the capacity to complete whatever it is he starts; he can be difficult to get along with, but is nevertheless reliable and thorough in all his undertakings. He prefers not to stray too far from the paths of accepted convention, and he behaves naturally and unaffectedly in whatever company he might find himself. There is no friction between his public and his private lives, neither being advanced at the expense of the other. He has come to terms with himself and has found fulfilment in his work. He is a complete professional, and he has combined his talent with hard work to achieve the success he so richly deserves.

'Thanks for your analysis; the whole account seemed to be quite accurate' — Gordon Honeycombe

John Arlott, OBE

Dear Mr Holmes,

It is somewhat late in life for me to give examples of my sprawling spider, but such as he is — ancient and weary

Best wishes,

Yours sincerely,

John Arlott

HANDWRITING HIGHLIGHTS

The many angles present in the writing clearly show that the writer can be a hard and awkward individual who relies on his own judgement and is not easily swayed by the opinions of others. The slant of the strokes to the right, and the way in which he extends many of the final strokes to the last letters of words, depicts his active social awareness and his need for contact with others.

The writing, when considered in its entirety, is strong; has aesthetic qualities; contains a degree of fussiness; and is well-balanced. All these features can also be attributed to the personality of John Arlott. The bars crossing the letter 't' are very strong, which confirms the earlier indications that this man is very self-reliant and unyielding in his approach to life. See how the stroke which underlines his signature ascends quite sharply: a clear sign that he feels well able to cope with life's difficulties.

PORTRAIT

As one would expect, John Arlott has a harmonious personality which makes him genuine in outlook as well as behaviour. He is a good speaker and stylist, as well as being efficient and capable in the spheres of everyday life. He evaluates things in a balanced way, carefully weighing up the pros and cons before giving voice to his well-informed opinions. There is both caution and conformity about the way in which he dresses, and indeed about the way in which he behaves, and there is a tendency to start worrying when he feels that a situation is not totally under his control. His mind is able both to examine new concepts and to indulge in periods of meditation, and there are strong feelings towards the outside world combined with a real need for human contact. There is an active social awareness and he enjoys meeting people and it seems that his main interests are centred on making social contacts and on developing rewarding personal relationships. But for all that, it is not easy for him to put his deepest inner feelings on display as he likes to keep them restrained and controlled. The disposition is firm, one might even say hard and awkward, and there is strong self-reliance plus an unyielding quality. He will act independently, and once he has taken up a stance he will remain true to it and not be afraid of any ensuing difficulties or problems. Persistent and ready to defend his point of view, he is not easily deflected from his chosen path. Certainly he is a man who likes to have his own way, and his active, imaginative mind is full of novel and constructive ideas which he is well able to express.

He has a liking for physical activity and a corresponding dislike of boring routine, so it is hardly surprising that travel is something he enjoys, becoming restless and dissatisfied if kept in one place for too long.

His public and private lives are in balance, neither being lived at the expense of the other, and there is a continuous expression of modesty and sincerity in both. He has come to terms with himself and with reality, and as a result he has found in his life a level of security. Harmony of the mind is sought and usually achieved by attempting only that which he feels is within his compass, and he conducts his affairs, be it in relation to time, emotion or finance, with considerable prudence. John Arlott has always been and in fact still is, one of life's umpires — firmly in control.

'Your analysis made me think very deeply of all the different influences in my handwriting, and they made my hair stand on end' — John Arlott

Jimmy Savile, OBE, HON. KCSG

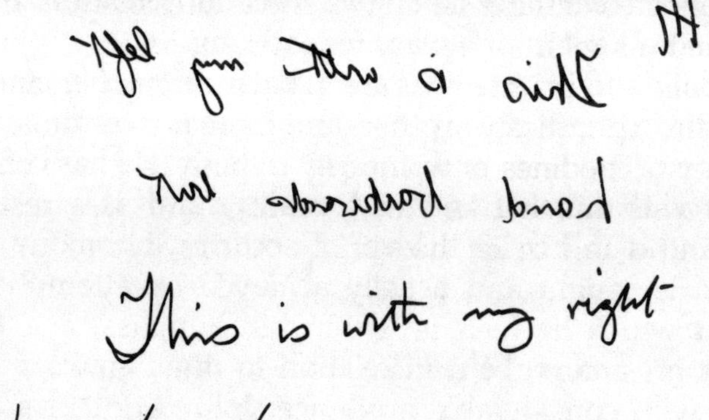

[handwritten mirror-writing text followed by:]

This is with my right hand forward.

Jimmy Savile [signature with smiley face]

HANDWRITING HIGHLIGHTS

The high IQ of this man is clearly demonstrated by the way in which he has dashed off the genuine mirror writing which so accurately shadows his normal script. It would appear that it is just as easy for him to write from right to left as it is to inscribe the words normally, and whilst this ability is usually associated with a disturbed psyche, there is no doubt that in the case of Jimmy Savile it is due to his uncommon intellectual capacity. There is pressure not only of the pen against the paper but also in the way letters are connected and this indicates his strength of will. There is also pressure applied across all three zones of the writing, which is a sign of leadership qualities and of a genuine wish to champion the underdog. Look at the face he has drawn in the lower loop of the capital 'J' in the signature: here we see his liking for the impressive and the ornamental, as well as his individuality of style. Legible writing points to his honesty of purpose, and strong bars crossing the 't's indicate an ability to stand fast in the face of adversity. The lines of writing slope upwards and this says quite simply that he has a positive and optimistic outlook and is able to lift the spirits of those around him.

PORTRAIT

Although Jimmy Savile needs to communicate with the outside world he has reservations as to exactly how much contact he should allow to keep it from impinging on his private life and on his independence. His extroversion, whilst healthy, is certainly not exaggerated, and when he deems it necessary he is able to resist outside influences and impose a meaningful pattern on his life. He has a great interest in the world but there is a conflict between his self-expressive and self-protective urges, and this can make his relations with others somewhat strained at times.

He is a determined man, relentless to himself and to others when in pursuit of his goals, and his activity at such time is of an exaggerated type, the energy, emotional intensity and willpower that he puts into it meaning that he usually achieves his aims. His never-resting mind is sensitive and not bound by the usual conventions, and his imagination is given free rein to have a great impact on him. The intense feelings are too strong to be bridled completely but the regulation of the impulses is quite good so he expresses only a minimum of nervous irritability and is, therefore, able to use his qualities in the most economical and purposeful way.

Confident and dominant in his relationships, he is able to strike up conversations with strangers quite easily, and is not put off by a discouraging initial response. He has a strong desire to behave according to his own needs and will defend himself vigorously when under attack. In a quarrel he will have few qualms about arguing his position openly, and defending his rights even on trivial matters. He is a zealous, competitive man with a powerful need to succeed in whatever he undertakes, and when pursuing a goal he can be intolerant towards those views that differ from his own, and at such time he can be a difficult man to contain. He is not particularly conformist and is intrigued by new ideas and situations, while routine for its own sake is tiresome to him and can make him moody and unpredictable.

He is an intellectual extrovert who requires freedom to express himself and there is an easy individual approach to matters of social and intellectual association. Although he has little time to stand and stare, he is nevertheless a man of soul and feeling, with a justified pride in his achievements and a strong materialistic tendency. In spite of the many adjustments that he has made he is still frequently disturbed by unexpected yearnings that are hard to define, but whatever the feelings of uncertainty, and there are some, he manages to keep them well suppressed and hidden.

There is a tendency for him to be rather impressionable; this he fights, but he still indulges in intellectual fantasies, although his gift of cold reasoning means that he is less influenced by them than others might be. So it would seem that in spite of his down-to-earth approach and his ability to cut the red tape, he is still influenced to some extent by conventional concepts and beliefs.

He is very much an individual who needs room to express himself, and who has a liking for the expressive and ornamental, and it is quite safe to say that he responds better to gentle persuasion than to coercion or sarcasm. There is a sensitivity of the feelings which is positive and controlled, making the personality well integrated and in tune with reality.

It is clear that Jimmy Savile is a man who can dream up ideas, take the initiative and then display the strength of purpose to finish what he starts. He is headstrong and wilful, and he can take some stopping when he gets the bit between his teeth. No appeal to his magnanimity will ever fail, as he genuinely sees his role as being a protector of the weak. He is a person of conviction, who, because he is prepared to stand by his beliefs, can in turn convince others, and since he has the strength to carry through his ideas, he also has the strength to overcome any opposition to those ideas.

Strongly emerging from the handwriting of Jimmy Savile is a leader with the practical psychologist's deep understanding of the creative and compassionate qualities that, hopefully, reside within us all.

Julian Lloyd Webber

To me the sound of the cello has a quite natural connection with the countryside, and no composer could have been more profoundly influenced by England's rolling landscape than Edward Elgar.

Julian Lloyd Webber

Right handed.

HANDWRITING HIGHLIGHTS

The unusual feature of this handwriting is the long swinging underlengths of the letters 'g' and 'y'. Although modified slightly in this writing, such strokes indicate hot temper, aggression, and an ability to fly off the handle at the slightest provocation. People who write in this way also tend to be uncompromising in their personal relationships and business dealings. There is aggression in the sharp bars crossing the letter 't', as well. Graphologically, the writing is slow and this states quite clearly that he is a calculating person who says very little without first giving the matter much thought, and intuitiveness is shown by the many disconnected letters. Good simplification of nearly all the letters is a sign of high intelligence, while the rising signature shows just how confident he feels about his ability to cope with any difficulties he might encounter.

The paraph under the signature is a forward and backward stroke and this means that he can give dramatic emphasis to an emotional moment.

PORTRAIT

The lively imagination of Julian Lloyd Webber is unconsciously and instinctively very active; in addition, it is no ordinary imagination, but rather the creative type with which artists of all persuasions are blessed. He also enjoys the wealth of his thoughts which, when connected with his art, become exaggeratedly vivid and creative. His powers of subjection and conception are stronger than the demands to adapt himself to that which is objectively necessary, and so he lives both through and for his music; in spite of this, however, there is no lack of clear reasoning.

He has a strongly developed emotional life, and both external impressions and his own thoughts have a great hold over him. His sensitive and never resting mind does not consider itself to be too tightly tied down by traditional forms, so that he has to exercise great control over his feelings if he is to channel them productively — all the signs pointing to them being too powerful to be completely curbed by will power; however, he can make them work for him only when they are concentrated on his love of music.

He finds it difficult to fit in with whatever is happening outside his immediate sphere of interest as he is invariably concentrating his mind on whatever task is currently engaging his attention. This difficulty in adapting comes from his need to express his creativity and individuality, so that when the freedom to do so is curtailed in any way he becomes aggressive and liable to show anger and frustration. At such a time it would take little provocation to incur his wrath and he would become uncompromising in both his personal relationships and business dealings. His instinct for self-protection is as strong as his need for self-expression, and the conflict between the two attitudes creates some stresses within the personality. Therefore, in spite of the many adaptations he might have made, his main difficulties are still not resolved, and he is quite often disturbed by hard-to-define longings and desires.

He is also a calculating person who says very little without first giving the matter much careful thought. The tongue is sharp and he is opinionated and wilful in his relations with others. He is not unduly influenced by the demands of those around him as he has confidence in his judgement and in his ability to cope with the problems and challenges of everyday life.

Great care is taken in his work, and his outlook and points of view are well balanced, making him practical and prudent, particularly in his personal affairs. There is so much happening in the mind of Julian Lloyd Webber and, with his behaviour being dictated by his cultural and artistic drive, he tends to have labels such as 'genius' and 'eccentric' applied to him — the truth is that this gifted and talented man is filled with creative urges that will not be denied, whatever the price he has to pay.

Derek Jameson

This is a subject I find most fascinating — and one day all the secrets of the universe will be revealed by those who push back the frontiers of knowledge in this way.

Derek Jameson

HANDWRITING HIGHLIGHTS

Spacing between lines and words is excellent and this shows that Derek Jameson had an orderly mind. The width of all the surrounding margins points to his insular nature; When hurt he retires inside himself. Hooks appear throughout on the end of strokes, indicating nervous energy and enthusiasm, while the many bent strokes that are open to the right show that he faces the future hopefully. Many angles go to make the letters and these are matched equally by arched or arcade forms comprising the majority of the letters 'n' 'm' and 'h'. Strength therefore is evident, but, more than that, there is hardness and an uncompromising approach. This man will not soften his line and opt for easy compromise if it means that he will lose his originality. The pen strokes are thick and sensuous in their appearance and this means that he is a man who lives his life through his senses, knowing instinctively what it is that makes people tick.

PORTRAIT

Derek Jameson does not waste time on non-essentials, having developed a direct approach to life, and he has absolutely no intention of compromising with the world if such compromise would cost him his originality. In fact, popularity for its own sake interests him not at all, and quite often he can be openly hostile to the demands of those around him. He has within him a strong need to be his own man and to do his own thing, and his strong conquest of the self has given him a firm personality, enabling him to concentrate upon what he is doing, even under difficult and trying circumstances.

Instinctive excitement and irritation are present in his make-up and he is not totally free from the influences of the past, which he might reject, but by which he still feels threatened.

He exercises good control over the emotions, and makes sure that his mind takes over at decision-making times. He is a vital man, definitely not easy to understand or to please, but there are no pretences, and he intensely dislikes superficial people, preferring forthright relationships in all spheres of his life. He can be inconsistent at times, seeing situations in detail one day and then generalizing about them the next, and he can vacillate between withdrawn solitude and excited sociability.

Whatever adjustments he might make to his life, he is nevertheless frequently disturbed by his unexpressed yearnings.

He does not always show the degree of confident fluency in his expressiveness of which he is capable, and such can be his absorption with the impression he is creating in the here-and-now that it is possible for him to misjudge a situation and run himself into trouble which, with a little more thought and care, he might have avoided. There is inordinate ego involvement so that he concentrates much upon himself, with little attention left to spare for others. A bluntness and lack of finesse mean that he can be needlessly uncooperative and obstinately determined to stand by his rights and principles, and he will impulsively do and say what he must even if it inconveniences and offends others and later gives him cause for regret. On occasion, he has difficulty in controlling his feelings; he might go along on an even keel for a while and then suddenly, without warning, show fury and temper. He is either totally for, or against, and this headstrong approach means that he can eliminate resistance to his ideas and carry them through to a conclusion.

Usually self-contained and somewhat aloof, he appears generally friendly, but he never lets anyone get too close to his real self, and, despite outward appearances, Derek Jameson is unlikely to be putting on show his real inner feelings. Without a doubt, this stubborn and aggressive man does not want to be obligated to, or indeed bossed about by, anyone. He is able to adapt to his environment, but this adaptability does not spring from his inner being – rather, it is something into which he has to force himself. Being cautious, he does not like to stick his neck out unless he feels that the climate favours him. This carefulness also shows in his prudent nature, making him unable to splash out easily, be it with time, money or emotion, and yet, even though he is economical by nature, he does not like to seem mean.

He does find it difficult to fit in, as do many creative personalities, and, being somewhat unconventional, he has a tendency to resent any form of restraint because he requires freedom of thought and action in his everyday activities. However, his cool aversion to restrictive routine is more than compensated for by his warm enthusiasm for the matters which really engage his interest and it matters not whether these be in work or leisure – all will be met with lively energy.

From his fertile mind comes a wealth of ideas, and he is able to make quick intuitive appraisals and assessments, and then reach usually correct conclusions without the need for too much reasoning. There is an abundance of nervous energy, and he cannot remain still for long; verbally or physically, he has to be up and doing, and his impetus is rarely if ever checked by strict control, so that nervous impatience will prevent him from elaborating on matters in too much detail.

The underlying nature is rather sensitive and not a little self-conscious, but he is able to exercise good self-control over these characteristics – this self-control reached through an outward display of elaborate behaviour that is by no means a spontaneous expression of his true self. In private or in public, he rarely lets himself go, and as a result he is not particularly easygoing; nevertheless Derek Jameson is very much a human being who lives and relies on his instincts and senses. There is much he has yet to accomplish, and, no matter how difficult and intolerant he might appear in his dealings with others, his handwriting clearly shows that he is infinitely more unforgiving towards his own shortcomings.

'*Absolutely spot-on*' — Derek Jameson

Henry Cooper, OBE, KSG

Dear Mr Holmes,

Please find enclosed three or four lines of my script for your appraisal. Also I'm left handed, look forward to seeing the results.

Yours sincerely

Henry Cooper

HANDWRITING HIGHLIGHTS

Hooks at the beginning and end of many strokes point to energy and tenacity, and the heavy pressure reveals the innate strength of the man. The starting or lead-in strokes, which seem to be used to prop up the first letters of many words, certainly show that he does not feel it necessary to challenge accepted authority. Many of the letters 'a' and 'o' have strokes that roof the letter, before the letter itself is formed, which feature in handwriting reveals that the writer is cautious and keeps private a part of himself. This is because he believes that to reveal it would be unacceptable to others. The close spacing of the letters indicates his controlled nature as does the upright nature of the letter strokes; although some strokes are left-slanting they can be discounted as they are penned by a left-handed person. The main body of the writing is legible, yet the signature is illegible, and this points to Henry Cooper wishing to get his message across but at the same time to maintain the privacy of his feelings and emotions. The nature of the writing is strong, reflecting durability in the writer, and a slightly uneven distribution of pressure shows that he can lose his temper, although that would be a rare event. Look at the last letter of virtually every word and see just how clearly it has been written: this is a sure sign of an honest and reliable individual.

PORTRAIT

You would not need to know Henry Cooper for very long to realize that he has a mature personality, but what you might not realize is that like most other people he experiences uncertainty and unrest in his make-up due to unfulfilled ambitions and desires. He is rather cautious and conformist in both dress and behaviour, and is also a worrier who likes to think that he is able to control any situation in which he might find himself; in other words he likes his head to rule his heart. His moods are generally fairly even and predictable, but on the rare occasion that he does let go, there can be a real show of anger and frustration.

The pride he has in his achievements is fully justified and whilst he is concerned about what others think of him he does resent any interference by them in his life. Mostly he succeeds in controlling his feelings and only occasionally does he allow himself to be lavish, whether with time, finance or emotion, but whilst he is economical in his actions he does not wish to be considered mean or parsimonious.

Tenacious and purposeful, he thinks and works rationally and consistently, and can sometimes be assertive, obstinate and even downright unobliging. Strong personality that he is, he likes to get down to essentials quickly, and only rarely does he leave unfinished that which he has started. The character is upright, a bit starchy, perhaps — but it must be said that he is transparently honest and his words are as clear and unambiguous as he is. The headstrongness can make him difficult to cope with and he is definitely not a soft touch, his shrewd, business-minded approach enabling him to drive a hard bargain. He has a sensible approach to business contacts and he will enthusiastically develop opportunity by keenly examining and exploiting all that is offered.

He lives by a strict code of ethics, understanding fully the difference between right and wrong in whatever situation he finds himself. He does sometimes procrastinate, but this tendency is not so dominant as to seriously impair his decision-making processes.

Often impatient with detail, he tends to dislike purely routine work. His appetite is robust; he is fond of travel, preferring to keep on the move and becoming restless when he finds himself confined to one place. He likes to stay with the people and things he knows best, and lives his life usefully according to the prescribed pattern. You might accuse him of being overcareful, but his handwriting reveals that he does not feel it necessary to challenge accepted authority. There is a part of Henry Cooper that only he understands and he keeps it from even his closest acquaintances. He is a tough nut and even if you broke through the outer layer you would find waiting for you just as strong an interior. He is what you would expect him to be, a very durable man.

'My wife thinks it's just like me and so do I' — Henry Cooper

Eamonn Andrews, CBE

It always strikes me as odd that if you're a Right-handed person - as I am - you are a left handed boxer - as I was.

Eamonn Andrews

HANDWRITING HIGHLIGHTS

Long lower loops to the letters 'g' 'y' and 'f', in addition to the use of capitals where lower case should be used, indicates a liking for physical activity. The intuitive nature is revealed by the many letters that stand apart from their neighbour; and the way in which strokes are taken from the bottom of the lower zone straight through to start the next letter at the top of the upper zone denotes stubbornness and an argumentative nature. The presence of hooks at the end of many strokes shows clearly that he had an abundance of nervous energy that engaged him in constant activity and made it difficult for him to relax. He was a stable and self-confident man, as can be seen in the evenness of height of the middle-zone letters.

PORTRAIT

Eamonn Andrews was a discreet, shrewd and diplomatic person with a great deal of human understanding in his make-up, and he displayed pleasant, hopeful traits with a mind always open to new ideas. Realistic and most certainly not a daydreamer, there was in him a strong urge towards the outside world.

There was a good sense of purpose, with consistent drive. His personal sphere dominated his everyday life, and as he had quite a powerful and positive personality with strong feelings he could be argumentative, needlessly uncooperative and determined to stand by his rights and principles. No surprise then that he relied largely on his own judgement and made up his own mind about issues of the day.

Fairly broadminded and quite generous, he was discriminating in his generosity, counselled wisely by his mature, reasoning approach. He felt a need to express his views freely, and being inclined towards extroversion he did not feel inhibited in any way. Although his general demeanour was one of friendliness you would rarely if ever have been made privy to his most intimate thoughts, his tendency having been to keep others at arm's length if their curiosity became too blatant. He could be moody, and there was in him a sensitivity about the fact that he had not always taken full advantage of opportunities that had been presented.

For much of the time he would go along on an even keel and display a calm and unruffled temperament until suddenly he would show temper and even fury: a sign that, beneath the air of self-confidence, there was some strain. He had a fairly conventional approach to life, and there was a fondness for routine and a dislike of change for what might appear to be its own sake. The private life was kept under wraps and rarely was the public side allowed to intrude.

In many ways he was an intense man, active and interested in what was taking place in the world around him. He took naturally to skills requiring the use of physical energy and a harmonious co-ordination of mind and muscle. There was impatience with detail and a lack of enthusiasm for routine work, although being versatile he was able to break the monotonous parts of a task by tackling their repetitive functions in a variety of ways, thus avoiding becoming tired of even the most boring of jobs. He would become restless when confined, as, with his abundant nervous energy, there was a need for almost continuous activity, and this made it very difficult for him to relax. And he was tense and talkative to the point where he could, if he was not very careful, monopolize a conversation.

As said right at the beginning, Eamonn Andrews was discreet, shrewd and diplomatic, and in addition he had a strong personality. Without doubt, he was a good man to have in your corner.

Roy Hudd

Dear Mr. Hollines Thanks for your letter.
I'm delighted to send you an example
of my handwriting — I am right
handed and look forward to
recieving your findings.

Yours sincerely,

Roy Hudd

HANDWRITING HIGHLIGHTS

The writing is narrow, which is a sign of strong self-control, and the letters being placed close together tells us that he does not let himself go easily. Long-swing lower loops speak of materialism, and strong bars to the letters 't' say that he is not easily swayed by new ideas or situations. Many angles in the writing clearly show that he is a tough character who meets trouble head-on and faces his responsibilities squarely. The emphasized middle zone tells that he is more interested in his daily work than in anything else, while the large signature indicates self-esteem and pride in his achievements. The first letters of words are formed without use of starting or lead-in strokes so it can be said that Roy Hudd is able to get to the heart of a matter quite quickly, dispensing with unnecessary preliminaries. The thick pasty lines tell us that he enjoys indulging his physical appetites and that he is an earthy and unrestrained individual. The height of the middle zone letters is quite constant throughout and this can only be achieved by someone who is stable and self-confident. In this positive script of good standard, the mingling of letters of one line with those of another speaks of versatility as do the wavy or serpentine lines of the writing.

PORTRAIT

The main interests of Roy Hudd lie with his work and it is quite clear that it is this aspect of his life which gives him most satisfaction. The man is a real livewire and his fertile brain is constantly germinating ideas. With his ability to focus his mind, he is able to separate the good schemes from the bad and pursue only those that have real potential. And when pursuing an idea, he will push himself and others unmercifully, which approach means that he is rarely if ever deflected from his chosen course, either by his own sympathies or by outside influences. Sometimes when he gets really fired up by a particular plan of action he finds himself driven more by impulse than guided by reasoning, but he is usually able to apply the brakes to his highly developed imagination and stop it running riot and affecting his ability to be objective.

He combines clarity of thought with originality when pursuing his activities and there is a readiness to reveal his thinking unreservedly as he has great confidence in his inspiration. This confidence can make him rather self-opinionated and wilful; to some he might appear forbidding and unobliging.

Exacting and efficient, there is within him a strong sense of justice and he tends to be concerned that he receives his dues when dealing with others. He does not make new friends easily — or perhaps a more correct interpretation of what is there in the handwriting is that he prefers old values, and loyally stands by those values that he acquired when young; values which still hold meaning for him; meaning which he still wishes to preserve.

Being somewhat dependent upon the approbation of others, he tends to overrate the social and material sides of his life at the expense of the intellectual, but this should not lead one to the conclusion that he has not been blessed with a keen intellect, for his mind is both original and imaginative.

He is a man of exaggerated activity and if he is unable to find an outlet for his energy then he becomes unsettled, argumentative and even quarrelsome. He is shrewd, and has a distinct liking for organizing his own affairs as well as those of others — but he certainly does not permit outside interference to affect his actions.

He enjoys indulging his physical appetites and he is an earthy, natural and unconstrained individual who enjoys the company of others; and whilst his behaviour leans towards the ostentatious it is nevertheless a true reflection of the real man. He is absorbed with the material and practical sides of life, and his aspirations in these areas are great. Justifiably proud of his achievements, he continues to live a full life which imparts to him much satisfaction.

When Roy Hudd mobilizes his talents he gives the impression of being an irresistible force and very little that stands between him and what he hopes to achieve would he for one moment consider immovable.

'Pretty good, and my friends tell me so too' — Roy Hudd

Naturalness

Natural writing emanates from natural people, who reveal their pleasant, rounded, easy-flowing personalities in letter forms that display similar characteristics. The real clue to their lack of pretension is in the style and size of writing of both the signature and the main body of the text. In every case they are identical. What you see of these people is what there is — no more and no less.

Marjorie Proops, OBE

Dear Mr. Holmes,

I am happy to send you this sample of my handwriting —

Sincerely

Marjorie Proops

HANDWRITING HIGHLIGHTS

Sincerity and a wish to be understood are shown by the legibility of the handwriting to be the major features of her personality. The large signature and flowing style of the script reveal her outgoing nature and a tendency towards exaggeration: flamboyance of character generally shows itself in handwriting that is large and full of strokes that serve no purpose other than that of embellishment. Strong bars to the letters 't' in this case tell of a strong will — there is no way that this lady will be pushed around. Initial letters are often larger than those that follow, indicating an ability to lead and take the initiative. The letters 'n' are formed with a wavy line, which indicates the inherent friendliness of her personality but there are a few angular strokes that counterbalance the kindliness with a firmness. Look carefully at the way she uses different ways of producing the same letter; this is a sure sign of versatility and creativity. Many connections are made using strokes that travel direct from the writing base line to the upper zone which clearly point to her being an intellectual extrovert. The top and bottom bars to the capital letters 'I' reveal her constructive, practical and businesslike approach to matters.

PORTRAIT

Marjorie Proops is warm-hearted, socially aware, adapts well to the needs of everyday life, and is above all else in tune with reality. She has a naturally receptive and friendly disposition with a balancing control of firmness, and she has the ability to understand the problems and difficulties of others.

There is a desire, one might even say a need, to be understood, as she is basically a sincere and unambiguous person who feels no need whatsoever to conceal any part of herself from others. She enjoys a natural relationship with the surrounding world, and is open to influences which can, if they impress her sufficiently with their worthwhile characteristics, have a profound effect upon her. Although she has a positive personality there is a preference for avoiding conflict whenever possible; nevertheless, her strong feelings and firm convictions give her the appearance of being headstrong and self-opinionated. She needs to express her individuality and to develop further the style which is all her own and to this end she uses rather flamboyant gestures and will if necessary gild the lily.

Energetic, active, and with wide-ranging interests, she obtains great joy from her life of action and enterprise. A mature and well-integrated personality makes her aware of the realities of everyday life, and this awareness is strengthened by a self-control which enables her to hold her emotions and feelings in check while she thinks things through carefully and thoughtfully. There is a temperamental impressionability which she disciplines quite well, and she is not easily swayed by new ideas or situations. There is good vision as well as an active imagination, and she is able to consider matters with a mind unfettered by material considerations — this can sometimes lead to her overrating the practical or sentimental aspects of life. Generally calm and reliable, she remains unruffled when others panic, and this clearly demonstrates the control she exercises over her inherently excitable temperament.

Marjorie Proops is not only able to conceive ideas but she is also able to take the initiative and carry them through to a conclusion. Her strength of character makes her thorough and reliable, but it can be mistaken for headstrongness, and can, on occasion, make her difficult to deal with. She is a protector of the weak and of the underdog and is always ready to espouse their cause; no appeal to her magnanimity would go unanswered. Through helping people she has put meaning not only into her own life but also into the lives of others, and by doing so she has found fulfilment.

'My assistant, Fiona, who knows me better than I know myself tells me it is amazingly accurate, including the self-opinionated and headstrong bit' — Marjorie Proops

Max Bygraves, OBE

Dear Mr Holmes.
                    As requested —
forgive the postcard am, rushing
to catch plane from Heathrow —
hope this will suffice.
                    Yours truly,
                    Max Bygraves.

HANDWRITING HIGHLIGHTS

An easygoing approach to life is clearly demonstrated
by the relaxed strokes and easy flow of the handwriting,
and if you trace the path the lines take you will find the
continuously undulating movement almost hypnotic in
its character. The rightward slant of the script in general
speaks of extroversion and the ability to reach out and
make contact with others. The writing is clearly legible,
which points to the sincerity of the man, as does the fact
that the letters in the signature are identical to those of the
main body of the text. The letters of the middle zone of the
writing are fairly constant in height throughout — a sign
of self-confidence — whilst the strong bars crossing the

letters 't' clearly show that he is a man who is not easily swayed by an untried concept. The final letter in every word is firmly and clearly written, an indication of reliability and dedication. The fact that he is able to balance his private life with his public life is evident in the way in which he shows no preference for either his first or last name, both being written with the same naturalness and without extra emphasis.

PORTRAIT

From the relaxed style of his writing, it is quite apparent that Max Bygraves does not have a white-knuckle approach to life. Rather, he is easygoing, though somewhat non-conformist with a liking for demonstrating his affinity with things which are different and unusual. He enjoys throwing himself wholeheartedly into a project which has captured his interest, and at such times he tends to shun the by-the-book approach, preferring spontaneity and improvisation; if unnecessary routine can be avoided then he will avoid it. It is obvious from the unrestrained nature and rightward slant of the writing that he is an extrovert, and as such he directs his energies outwards towards the world, people, and future goals. His impulsiveness can sometimes cause him to say and do things which he will almost certainly regret. He is emotionally responsive and, with reactions that are spontaneous and born of self-confidence, he is well able to form and cement successful relationships. It is this emotional responsiveness which gives him the ability to capture the hearts of an audience. To make him give of his best he needs constant stimulation — thus at a social gathering you would see him move from person to person giving just a little time to each rather than spending all evening talking to one or two. His moods tend to fluctuate because of his emotionality, and as a result scenes are not uncommon;

their effects, however, are short-lived, as he forgives and forgets very quickly. His desire to be understood by others and the words he utters are as sincere as his character is transparent. He is considerate of the feelings of others and can adjust himself to the demands of the world, the conditions of his work, and his social life. Well able to take the initiative in his dealings with others, his mind is in tune with reality and this gives him a well-balanced outlook.

He processes his ideas in a logical manner, and this makes him practical; his imagination is disciplined, and when this is added to the practicality there results a shrewdness which enables him to understand the basic elements of a situation, so that when necessary he is able to drive a hard bargain. Versatile in his approach, he is able to break the monotony of any repetitive task by introducing novel features into his actions. He has quite a penetrating insight into human relationships and activities, which helps him to establish connections with others, but in spite of this there is some emotional reticence and this makes him play some of his cards close to his chest. He might give the appearance of being totally outgoing and spontaneous, but you can be quite sure that he keeps something of himself in reserve.

Generally, his behaviour is forthright, and there are strong convictions and a fixity of purpose that make him quite capable of defending his views and principles. He does not feel in any way restricted by feelings or inhibitions from the past, and the result is he has a strong purpose in life.

He does not shirk or avoid his responsibilities and he will tackle a problem head-on rather than put it off to a later date. He is not influenced too easily by new ideas although his interest is easily aroused and he will keenly examine what is on offer. One could describe his approach as radical thought tempered by conservative action.

He has managed to balance the demands of his career with those of his private life, giving prominence to neither.

There is little if any pretentiousness or ostentation in his make-up, although there is some vanity and he does tend to be rather self-approving — but really there is no more of these traits than should be expected from someone who is genuinely talented and successful.

The man is natural, what you see is what he is . . . there is neither more nor less beneath the surface. There is also moderation, and generally he does not strive after things which are outside his range and beyond his control; and this attitude allows him to bring happiness not only into his own life but also into the lives of others.

The handwriting of Max Bygraves reveals that he has got his act together in every sense of the phrase.

'I feel your assessment of my character is pretty accurate'
— Max Bygraves

Jean Alexander

Dear Mr. Holmes,

Thank you for your
letter. Herewith the example
of handwriting you requested.
I am right handed!

Yours sincerely,

Jean Alexander.

HANDWRITING HIGHLIGHTS

Adaptability, moderation, objectivity and the ability to combine clarity of thought with originality are all indicated by the legibility of the writing and the way in which few strokes of letters descend far below or rise much above, the writing line.

There is simplification of letter forms, pointing to good basic intelligence, and strong connecting strokes between the letters are a sign of sense of purpose. Kindness and consideration are featured in the wavy formations of the letters 'h' 'n' and 'm'; while the basic similarity of the letter shapes in the signature with those of the rest of the writing clearly shows that Jean Alexander is a natural and unaffected person.

If you examine carefully the way she joins one letter to another you will see that shortcuts are taken without affecting the legibility. This is indicative of the fluency and adeptness that is within her personality.

PORTRAIT

There is a slight degree of reserve and possibly even caution to be observed in Jean Alexander, which would be particularly noticeable on first acquaintance; however, it would not be long before her confidence was won, so allowing the more spontaneous person that she keeps hidden to emerge. She has a gentle nature and a peaceable temperament, and she shows consideration towards the needs of others. There is an instinctive sympathy which gives rise to an attitude of tolerance towards both people and situations. She will not argue a point for the sake of argument, and is able to adapt her well-integrated personality to see both sides of a disagreement.

There is an inner strength which she applies to whatever it is she is doing and this provides her with consistency in her work. As she is rarely carried away by her feelings she is not inclined to waste energy on matters that are superfluous to the main stream of her activities, and can therefore put her talents to the best use.

She is mentally active, and altogether a fluent and articulate person, in whom the freedom to express herself is a must, and if she finds herself restricted by the dictates of another she is well able to talk herself out of the situation. Likes and dislikes are usually formed on first impression, and she is an extremely difficult person to deceive.

She is rather a spendthrift when it comes to travel and clothes, but, in most spheres of life, being both intelligent and sincere, she is a woman of moderation, matter-of-factness and objectivity, which qualities she combines with her clear thought and originality to make her well adapted to work and circumstances in general.

There is an ability to think in the abstract, and her imagination and intelligence enable her to fulfil her ambitions; and, as she has come to terms with the reality of her life, there is a feeling of achievement that gives her much satisfaction. There are strong ethical tendencies which, when combined with her well-balanced outlook, make her realistic, business-minded and trustworthy. Her word is her bond.

Jean Alexander has an inner maturity and an ability to move in the various areas of her life in an easy manner without wasting her energies. She is a moderate and a modest person who has no desire to venture beyond that which she understands and feels capable of achieving. It is because of this that she is able to bring pleasure and comfort into her own life and, perhaps more importantly, it gives her the capacity to bring pleasure and happiness into the lives of others.

'Your reading is so accurate that it is hard to believe that you don't know me personally' — Jean Alexander

John Timpson, OBE

Dear Mr Holmes—

Thank you for your letter about your forthcoming book on graphology. I hope this is a sufficient sample of my handwriting, and I shall be interested to see what you make of it. I am incidentally right-handed.

Yours sincerely,

John Timpson.

JOHN TIMPSON.

HANDWRITING HIGHLIGHTS

Good legibility and soft, rounded letter-formations clearly indicate that the writer has a pleasant, well-integrated personality. Reasoning and logic as well as sound judgement are revealed in the connectedness of the script, while the strength of the strokes that tie the letters together point to his purposeful approach to work. The top of certain letters such as the 'd' and 'w' curve back to the left, which is a sign that introspection is present in the character. Although a felt pen has been used, the writing is nevertheless pasty, the majority of strokes being of an equal thickness throughout their length. This is the writing of a man who relies on his senses and who revels in the fulfilment of his physical appetites.

The middle zone dominates the writing and this points to his desire to work within his limitations.

John Timpson objects to being classed as a pleasant person, but really there is nothing in the handwriting to indicate otherwise.

PORTRAIT

Examination of the handwriting of John Timpson reveals a man with an extremely well-integrated personality, who additionally is in tune with the realities of his everyday life. Furthermore, he is a person who weighs events and happenings on the scales of careful consideration so that the views and opinions he holds are rounded-out and well-balanced.

He is particularly interested in what is taking place in the world around him and not only does he understand how events are connected but he can clearly and precisely explain the connection to others. From this it can be seen how important it is to him to get his message across to others, to which end he is greatly assisted by the clarity of his thought and the lucidity of his expression. His reasoning is good and his judgement sound, which means that he is able to sum up situations quickly and correctly; add to these qualities the fact that he is a natural-born organizer, then it is not difficult to understand that he is not the type to get in a panic when the pressure is on.

There is some introspection and self-enquiry, but both are well disciplined and turned to positive use: nevertheless, he does like to keep the world at arm's length — not because he wishes to escape from the responsibilities of life, but because he wants to use his individual qualities more effectively and to enjoy the tranquillity that comes from doing what is right for him. There is also about him the indefiniteness of the many-sided personality, which means that he remains fluid and adaptable towards any new situation, and open-minded towards any new concept. He does of course recognize the desirability of avoiding ambiguity but none the less he feels that it is not in his best interest to be committed too deeply to one line of thought — in simple terms, he is a man who likes to keep his options open for as long as possible.

Once he has decided on a course of action, he plunges into the middle of things without too many preliminaries and uses intelligent effort to get to the heart of a matter. He likes to avoid extremes and leans towards concentration and self-imposed restriction, rarely venturing beyond that which he feels is outside his control. These traits are so dominant that it would be reasonable to say that he is devoted to the saving of time and effort.

Unaffected and with a modest nature, he abhors superficiality in all its guises, but he is also conscious of the need for form and deportment, and always exercises in his affairs good taste and a sense of proportion. He has a real sympathy for the plight of those less fortunate and he is blessed with a peaceable temperament and a liking for order and method. His aims, ideals and physical drives are therefore rarely in conflict.

He can be uneasy when working on his own, and functions best when in the company of others as he requires external stimuli to assist in developing his ideas. John Timpson relies a great deal on his senses, living much through what he sees and hears, and there is so little discord in his make-up that he would seem to be one of the few people who gain great satisfaction from their life and work.

Richard Todd

I hope that your book will
be a great success.
I am right - handed.
Richard Todd.

HANDWRITING HIGHLIGHTS

The impulsive nature of the writing reveals that characteristic within his personality, and the hooks appearing at
the beginning and end of many strokes reflect his nervous
energy.

Sociability is indicated by the rightward-slanting
strokes, and a basically easygoing nature is shown by
the wide space left between many of the letters. The
straight lines of writing tell of his equanamity and the
strong bars to many of the letters 't' show that he is not
a man to be swayed easily by the opinions of others.

The christian name and the surname are written iden-
tically, which means that his private and public lives are
in balance, while the fact that the lettering of the signature is identical to the main body of the writing means that
he is natural and unpretentious, with a strong dislike of

affection in others. The general layout is not too good, a sign that he still has much left to accomplish.

PORTRAIT

With a lively cultured mind and an enthusiastic nature, Richard Todd is a person of nervous energy who enjoys physical activities and leans quite positively towards being a doer rather than a theorizer. A short time after meeting him you would be aware of the inner enthusiasm that is born of his imagination, and he would appear tense and talkative with a marked inability to relax and unwind. Set him a task requiring the use of his creativity and you would make him happy, but recognize also that his emotionality is quite strong and that this can make him moody. There is an impulsiveness and some unpredictability, and he is quite capable of saying and doing things on the spur of the moment and afterwards wishing that he had been a little more thoughtful.

Basically, he is a realist, and, being preoccupied with the present, he rarely indulges in the luxury of daydreaming. His sense of purpose is well developed, and he will persist with an idea which attracts him, virtually to the extent of pig-headedness; as he feels strongly about his ideas, he will defend them volubly and to the point where one might say that he is fond of having the last word. He can, though, occasionally view life with a certain amount of inconsistency, looking at a subject in detail one day and generalizing about it the next.

The imagination is blended in well with the intelligence so that he can put his vision to good use and develop his ideas in an orderly and logical manner. He is discreet and diplomatic, and any doubts he might have about life are kept well hidden. Generally, the urges are self-expressive, but he will nevertheless pause before taking a calculated risk; his dominantly positive and optimistic outlook will, however, encourage him rapidly to override his natural caution. Overall, he tends to take things in his stride and prefers to learn from experience.

He is definitely a social being with a strong desire for contact with people, and there is a tendency to exaggerate the importance of social life at the expense of intellectual needs. His relationships with others do, however, appear to have a rather competitive edge to them, due to the partly suppressed aggression in his make-up which also accounts for his sense and, indeed, need for the dramatic moment. As he is adaptable, he is able to express his emotions in a sensitive and positive way, and, with his instinctive understanding of the human condition, combined with his warm, outgoing approach to others, it is not too surprising that he is a good entertainer.

There is little if any pretension, and his consideration for others as well as his sincerity are outstanding features of the writing. This mature personality achieves and maintains a harmony of the mind by staying with what he knows and does best, and this disposes him towards contentment and happiness.

When one examines the overall character of Richard Todd it would appear that he is well suited to play a leading and successful part in the game of life.

Kathy Staff

Dear Derek,
        Thank you for your letter of June 4th.
        I feel very pleased that you have decided to include me in your book and hope this is what you want — written by my right hand.
                        Yours sincerely,
                        Kathy Staff.

HANDWRITING HIGHLIGHTS

The gentle legible writing reflects a sincere and considerate personality, and her fondness for people as well as her uncomplicated outlook on life is shown by the medium pressure of her pen on paper.

There is a fine zonal balance about the writing, and to achieve this there has to be a peaceable temperament, and a love of order and method. From the above features it would be correct to assume that her aims, ideals and physical drives are not in conflict.

The fact that she is guided by feeling rather than reasoning is shown by the narrow spacing between words, while the rounded writing is a sign of pliable emotions and an instinctive sympathy that gives rise to tolerance. The wavy lines used to form the letters 'n', 'm' and 'h' indicate both her readiness to help others and her striving to avoid conflict. That she prefers to follow conventional paths is shown by the general connectedness of the writing.

PORTRAIT

The handwriting of Kathy Staff clearly indicates her peaceable temperament and her love of order and method. Her aims, ideals and physical drives are not in conflict, which enables her to exercise a sense of proportion over all that she does. She likes to establish a routine as she is not too fond of change, and her approach to matters tends to be conventional and well-balanced. She is considerate of the feelings of others and sincere in her approach to all things, and as there are no violent emotions she remains unprejudiced, impartial and objective towards events. She is also very careful in her work, carrying out tasks in a most reliable and conscientious way.

She is fundamentally a feeling person with pliable emotions and an instinctive sympathy which gives rise to tolerance. She is inclined to hide her thoughts and emotions, and when this trait is combined with her rather intuitive tendencies we find that she is able to sum up a situation quickly without getting into a panic.

She is ambitious, but not in a way that disturbs her equilibrium. Nevertheless she does wish to achieve something lasting, but neither success nor failure would basically affect her fundamental approach to life.

She is fond of people, and is the possessor of an uncomplicated personality, which makes her kind and with a readiness to help others, but she is not a sentimental or conciliatory person. She has a natural relationship with the surrounding world and is always open to external impressions, with the result that she can be influenced by the views of others.

She has a social conscience and her life is strongly influenced by spiritual, emotional and social forces.

A practical person who is extremely prudent in her personal affairs, Kathy Staff has been able to combine successfully the demands of her professional career with those of her private life. The equable way in which she has accomplished this clearly demonstrates her harmonious temperament.

'A pretty fair assessment of my wife' — John Staff

Jill Gascoine

I have two signatures — one I do for lists —
This is it — Jill Gascoine
This I sign — Jill V gascoine
Right-handed

HANDWRITING HIGHLIGHTS

As shown by the strong well-balanced rhythm of the writing, she is well able to show her feelings in a controlled yet sensitive manner. The majority of the letters slant to the right and this indicates that she reaches out to make contact with others, but there are sufficient upright strokes to be assured that her head rules her heart. Her mental processes are continuous and she is far more likely to rely on logic than on intuition, as is revealed by the way in which she joins together most of her letters. Good taste and a sense of proportion are indicated by the well-formed and -sized capital letters. Here and there some letters appear that are small when compared with the majority of those in the script, and these point to feelings of insecurity, but as they are quite well concealed within the framework of the overall writing, it means that her uncertainties are well hidden from the outside world.

She is spontaneous, and adept at what she does, as is clearly seen from the fluency visible, for example, in the

way the bars to many of the letters 't' appear in the form
of a tick.

PORTRAIT

Jill Gascoine has a well-developed mind and a pliable nature that enables her to use her sensitive emotionalism in a
creative manner. Her personality is well put together and
she is in tune with her life and its realities. Her reactions
towards events are spontaneous, fluent and efficient, and
she looks outwards towards others and is prepared to be
friendly, affectionate and demonstrative towards them.
Her relationships with other people are extremely important to her as their reactions are the yardstick by which
she measures her own worth and her success. There
is nevertheless some reserve in her character and she
dislikes wearing her heart on her sleeve, so when the
occasion demands, her head is quite capable of ruling
her heart.

   She has a real need to be understood and here she is
helped by her clarity of thought and expression. Con-
versely, she understands other people and as a result is
well able to relate to them.

   She can take the initiative in a matter, and has the
strength of purpose to finish whatever she starts. As she is
wilful and headstrong, she can be 'a bit of a handful', and
her convictions being strong, she will stand her corner in
any disagreement. She is reliable and thorough in what
she does, and will respond readily to any cry for help as
there is sufficient strength in her make-up for the needs
of others. Her mental processes are continuous, she has
the necessary mental coordination to help her attain her
objectives, and she is the kind of person who relies far
more on logic than on intuition, all of which traits make
her a rational person, mature in outlook and practical by
nature.

As a rule she has her emotions well under control, but not so well controlled that it makes her responses to a situation rigid and automatic. Again, we return to the fluency of her character, which prevents her from being clumsy and unresponsive by compelling her to avoid following set rules of approach and behaviour. She is without doubt a warm-hearted person of taste and originality and her lively imagination is unconsciously and instinctively active. Outspoken she might be, but she certainly knows when tact is called for. Beneath her rather calm exterior there are some feelings of uncertainty and insecurity, but they also come under her firm control and are not allowed to interfere with her decision-making processes. There is therefore a conflict between the desire to graze on pastures new and the wish to preserve that which she has so far achieved; with her outgoing personality, though, the adventurous part of her is usually victorious. She quite enjoys organizing her own affairs but only rarely does she attempt to organize the affairs of others.

Whilst her private life is based on spontaneity, her professional sphere is subject to far more control. She finds it much easier to relax at home with her family and friends than she does at work, where she feels she still ..as something to prove. There is, however, no discord between her two lives and she behaves in the same natural way towards either.

The personality of Jill Gascoine is based on a harmonious blend of her private and her professional lives, and it is difficult to see where one begins and the other ends.

'Your analysis of my handwriting is amazingly accurate even though you found out I was insecure!' — Jill Gascoine

June Whitfield, OBE

Dear Mr. Holmes,

Thank you for your letter.

Here is a sample of my handwriting. Best wishes for your book.

Yours sincerely,

June Whitfield.

HANDWRITING HIGHLIGHTS

In this positive handwriting, the presence of irregular pressure shows that there is vitality, impulsiveness and resolution within the personality. Both words and letters are legible and original, allowing us to say that she can combine clarity of thought with originality. The openness of the script describes honesty and sincerity, but caution is voiced by the narrowing left margin. The letters 'a' and 'o' are formed with a fullness that is representative of the warm-hearted, as well as those with generous pliable emotions. The writing is not only full, it is also simplified, and this means there is a homogenous mixture of intelligence and imagination which allows her to put her ideas into effect. The spacing is fairly orderly between the words but not so between the lines, from which it may be deduced that her everyday life is quite well organized whilst the more worldly side of her life is less so. If you look at the writing on the line and that above and below, you will find that it appears quite uniform. This zonal balance can only come from someone who has a peaceable approach to, and a liking for, life. This equanimity stems from steadfastness, which is shown by the strong straight lines of writing.

PORTRAIT

The writing of June Whitfield is an expression of her inner strength and maturity, and clearly shows her ability to take an active interest in many spheres of life without overtaxing herself. As a result there is much contentment and happiness. Her personality is positive, and there are strong feelings that are reasonably well controlled, which gives her a balanced outlook on life. Being a realist, she is usually able to remain calm when others around her become agitated, and she is purposeful and systematic in her approach to her work, which she pursues steadily and to good effect. Being a natural and down-to-earth person, she is not easily influenced by new ideas until they have been subjected to her rational thought processess. She is an assertive person who approaches situations directly, and has the ability to eliminate the unnecessary and the irrelevant from her thinking.

Self-discipline gives a good control of her feelings, and this enables her to harness her talents and abilities in the fulfilment of her aims, but the self-discipline does occasionally break down, with resultant moodiness and irritability. She is sincere and warm-hearted, trying, wherever possible, to avoid hurting the feelings of others. Her emotions are pliable, and as she enjoys meeting people she is able to display towards them her love of life. Obliging, and open to the influences of those around her, she is quite capable of being impressed by their views, and as she is natural and spontaneous she also prefers to avoid conflict whenever possible. Although she enjoys being with others she is able to enjoy her own company and will benefit from periods of solitude and quiet.

Her imagination is tempered with sound powers of reasoning which give her the necessary mental co-ordination to achieve her goals, and because she relies on logic and reason this makes her a systematic thinker. There is also vitality, impulsiveness, and resolution, plus a blend of creative imagination and brains to give her the facility to make enough of her hopes a reality.

She has good taste and a sense of proportion, which gives her a well-balanced outlook and the ability to appraise everyday events objectively and accurately, and she has a liking for order in her affairs. She is thus well able to organize everyday matters, but in the more worldly side of her affairs she is not so sure of herself and there have been times when the resulting insecurities have prevented her from developing herself as fully as she would have wished. There is therefore some dwelling on what might have been, but she nevertheless has a confident, optimistic approach to life. She has made her career fit her private life, which she values highly, and neither interferes with the other. There is nothing at all pretentious about June Whitfield, and neither does she hide away any part of herself from her public or her friends.

Percy Thrower

HANDWRITING HIGHLIGHTS

This writing is concentrated on the middle zone, an indication that Percy Thrower limited himself to a definitely circumscribed field of activity. The uneven pressure pattern points to moodiness and irritability, although these facets of his character did not predominate. Letters are close spaced, which fact shows that he was not an easygoing man.

Legibility is quite poor, and with the negative features present in the script, it indicates his lack of consideration for others, while the simplification of letters shows that he developed a direct approach with little time to waste on matters he considered unimportant. The triple underlining beneath the writing indicates that here was a man who liked to have the last word and intended to go his own way regardless. The strokes are mainly the same thickness throughout, which is called pasty writing; people who form their letters in this way are usually the earthy type, near to, and with a love of, nature.

PORTRAIT

Percy Thrower was a man who concentrated on his work, went his own way and developed his own ideas. He was not a particularly considerate person, and away from his work found it difficult to relax. He developed a direct approach to what he did, and wasted little time on things that he considered of no importance. He confined himself to a definitely circumscribed field of activity, and excelled in the careful observation of detail. His thoughts were quite consistent, and he was generally systematic and purposeful in the way he worked, with a realistic and down-to-earth outlook on everyday life. He responded to difficulties and problems by using logic, and this, combined with his commercial instinct, made him business-minded, with a methodical way of handling finance. He kept his own counsel, rarely speaking until he had considered all aspects of a subject. His mind was orderly, well-organized and able to resist outside influences, although new ideas and concepts fascinated him and he usually examined them thoroughly.

He was a tactful, reserved and restrained man with a real understanding of people, who tended to be rather embarrassed by questions of a personal or emotional nature. Modest, reflective and philosophical in outlook, he was usually in control of his feelings and impulses, and invariably unwilling to let himself go. Mentally active and versatile, he was able to plan ahead whilst working at the day's requirements. He was willing and able to take the initiative in an enterprise, and there was ambition in his make-up, although it was not an unreasoning force. He wished to achieve something worthwhile, but had no wish to jeopardize either his peace of mind or his security.

The basic temperament was somewhat excitable, and although generally well controlled, irritability, moodiness and outbursts of temper were not unknown, some even developing to a point where he could become coercive.

He was able to deal with repetitive and boring tasks by varying his approach to them, and lived a life of some fulfilment with a fair degree of security by establishing, and then working to, a routine. There were few if any pretensions and what you saw was what he was — a natural man, near to life and nature, relying on and living through, his senses.

To summarize: Percy Thrower was a person who could think up new ideas and then set about putting them into effect, and once he had started a task he would see it through to a conclusion. He tended to go his own way and do his own thing, his character being rather inflexible, and held many strong views, usually about his work, and would stoutly defend them. His success was hardly surprising, with the rootstock being so strong that virtually any idea grafted on to it would take root and grow.

'I thought it was most interesting, as did my wife and other members of the family' — Percy Thrower

Nicholas Parsons

Dear Mr Holmes,

Thank you for your letter.
I was interested to hear about your book
on Graphology, and hope these few lines
will help. I was born left handed, but
was taught to write with my right hand.
This probably contributed to the stutter I
developed as a youngster.

Please show me anything
before printing for approval.

Best Wishes

Yours Sincerely

Nicholas Parsons

HANDWRITING HIGHLIGHTS

Many letters are embellished unnecessarily in a way that
does not improve the legibility or appearance of the writing, and this points to a fussiness and a tendency to dwell
overmuch on somewhat irrelevant and unimportant matters. The upper loops of letters such as 't' 'h' and 'l' are
quite round and inflated, which indicates a tendency to

fantasize and daydream. Many letters are not connected in any way to their neighbour, pointing to intuitiveness in the make-up. The bars that cross the letters 't' are strong, a sign of self-reliance. Many first letters of a word are taller than those that follow which clearly relates to his ability to take the initiative in matters of business. Sharply pointed strokes, and there are plenty of these, show that he has a sharp tongue and can be quite sarcastic when provoked.

Although the writing appears to be confused at first glance, it is clear that he has brought order to it; and the fact that the signature is identical to the rest of the script means that the face he shows to the world is a genuine one.

PORTRAIT

Nicholas Parsons is motivated by a deep longing to make something of his dreams, so it follows quite naturally that there is enthusiastic exploration and development of opportunity. He is a well-balanced person, sincere and with a fairly transparent character, and his developed mind and pliable nature mean that he has a realis-tic approach to everything he does. There is some temperamental impressionability, but he has learned to impose a relatively firm control upon his character, so that he usually appears rather cool and matter-of-fact. The reality is that there is a desire for change and variety so that in spite of the control he applies he is frequently disturbed by longings for things yet to be accomplished. At such times he can be moody, but he soon reasserts himself, once again to direct his energies in a creative manner. His high ideals of personal attainment are also an incentive to self-discipline.

There is a nervous energy and an inner enthusiasm which emanate from his imagination, and the demands these make force him into continuous activity, making him tense, enthusiastic, active and talkative. Sometimes his dreams will intrude into reality, causing him to become impatient with himself and others; then, of course, he will experience difficulties connected with the people to whom he has shown impatience, and he will appear somewhat unsociable and possibly uncompromising. The problem here is also that people rarely live up to his preconceived idea of what they should be, and this tends to disappoint him.

His is not a particularly logical mind; rather it is able to make quick appraisals and assessments in an intuitive way. There is, however, an abundance of ideas which he is able properly to associate and relate to, and whilst at times he might appear to be detached, he has in reality a sharp and discerning mind. He can be off-hand towards those tasks that he feels restrict him, but for those jobs which really interest him he reserves a considerable amount of warm enthusiasm. He is able to provide solutions to problems because he can readily separate the essential from the non-essential, which he does with adroitness and intelligence, although he can on occasion be rather fussy and over-conscientious. He can work just as easily towards a goal a long way ahead or towards some more immediate aim, in either case confident of accomplishing what he has set out to do. He has good energy and verve, which he combines with pleasant hopeful traits and a constantly optimistic view of the future. Imagination and idealism drive him towards his lofty goals, which have usually to do with his social aspirations, and here he is aided by his cultured taste andd intellectuality which have developed within him a sense of form and deportment. Convention plays a very important part in his life.

Nicholas Parsons is, therefore, a man who likes to adhere to conventional habits, concepts and beliefs; has a keen, alert interest in matters generally; is sometimes fussy about things which do not really matter; does not allow himself to be influenced too easily by new ideas or situations and is purposeful and determined. He is not at all pretentious, and his private and public lives are fairly well balanced although he does favour his private life. There is some anxiety in the make-up, and he tends to look to the past as a means of trying to ascertain the values of the present and the future. He has come to terms with himself in relation to reality and has regulated his life to useful purpose, finding a measure of security in the face of change by planning his life in accordance with established practice. He does find it difficult to display his inner feelings and emotions because of his uncertainty about people, but when the occasion demands he is well able to put on a show of friendliness.

In spite of what you might think, you will rarely if ever catch sight of the real Nicholas Parsons which, in view of what has been revealed of him through his handwriting, seems rather a shame.

'I am truly impressed with your skill and ability. What has amazed me is the accuracy of the portrait from reading only a few lines of my handwriting' — Nicholas Parsons

Originality

People who are very original in both their outlook and achievements usually write fairly or extremely illegibly. Letters take on the most unusual shapes as the writer has no desire whatsoever to be 'understood'. Many letters and even whole words, when taken either in or out of context, are extremely difficult if not impossible to read. There is no way that these writers will compromise with the world if there is any danger of them losing their originality. They are the awkward people, the nonconformists in society and it is them we must thank for much of the variety in the world.

David Jacobs

Dear Derek Holme.

Here is the sample of my handwriting as requested in your letter of June 9th.

I am in fact right handed & feel that my writing changes not only according to the pen that I am using, but how interested I am in what I am doing & also how tired I am!

Yours [signature]

DAVID JACOBS.

HANDWRITING HIGHLIGHTS

Although somewhat irregular, the writing is nevertheless quick and even — an indication of these characteristics in the personality of the writer. Right and left tendencies or impulses in the upper zone of the script point to his mind being both speculative and reflective, and the tasteful presentation shows that he possesses aesthetic qualities. The writing is fairly rigid, which would mean he is cautious in his approach to others as well as being a man who hides his deepest feelings. The right slant of letters is a sign of his liking for people as well as his great social awareness. Connectedness of the writing points to a logical mind and a reasoning way of dealing with matters, but intuitiveness is present, as shown by the occasional breaks between letters.

The pressure is medium and the pattern even, indicating vitality and a love of people. The different ways he has of forming the same letter speaks volumes for his creativity, and the way in which he links his first name and surname clearly states to the analyst that he is a particularly distinctive individual. Letter simplification is diverse, and this demonstrates good basic intelligence and the ability to get down to the essentials of a subject.

PORTRAIT

The working speed of David Jacobs is quick, even and reliable and only rarely is he carried away by his feelings and impulses. Knowing how to employ his energies most economically means that he wastes little time on trivialities. He does not like to feel confined but this can happen because there is a tendency for him to think faster than he is able to express himself, and at such times he becomes moody and irritable.

His mind is speculative and thoughtful, and he possesses good powers of observation and concentration. He is well able to think in the abstract, and altogether those thoughts are orderly and well organized. There is a developed critical sense which inclines him towards intellectual aggressivenesss and authoritarianism, but his sense for the essential is nevertheless developed tastefully, and there is a strong urge to present things aesthetically. If you spent time in his company you would find that he is a rather restrained individual and somewhat cautious and conventional in his approach to issues, for he is quite concerned as to what others think of him. He is conformist in his judgement regarding everyday matters and in the way he copes with situations, and he will, in the main, accept conventional expressions of authority.

Generally even-tempered and dependable, he has good powers of concentration and is good at working at tasks requiring attention to detail, although his temper can get a bit short, particularly when he is engrossed in the travails of a new project. A creative person, he is well adapted to his work and his surroundings, and has a strong desire to be independent. He is socially very aware, and experiences few if any difficulties when meeting people, and in general he enjoys their company. Although he is self-contained, there is a need to share his feelings, but he finds it most difficult to display openly his deepest desires, and he will usually deal with them by denying their very existence. He has some difficulty in accepting logical conclusions made by others if they conflict with his own rather dogmatic views and opinions, but this rather blinkered approach is in reality a defence against the fact that he is somewhat impressionable and rather easily influenced.

There is some daydreaming, occasionally bordering on the neglect of reality, but this is due to the strength of his creative urges. David Jacobs is primarily a thinker, with a complex and interesting mind which is the foundation of his distinctive and very individualistic approach to life.

'My wife thinks that in the main it is very accurate' — David Jacobs

Willie Rushton

A lump of 'Shropshire Lad'
_____

And I shall find some girl perhaps
And a better one than you,
With eyes as wise but kindlier,
With lips as soft, but true,
And I daresay she will do.

Nothing personal. Yours Willie Rushton

HANDWRITING HIGHLIGHTS

The darting strokes reveal the quick-thinking characteristics of his alert brain, while the simplification of letters depicts the high level of intelligence. A lack of lead-in or starting strokes to the first letter of each word clearly shows that he has a direct approach to life. The arched or arcade strokes which form the letters 'h' 'n' 'm' point to the importance of form and deportment in his life, and the conflicting left to right stroke slants show the conflict within his psyche.

Great sensitivity and originality is contained within the writing, and versatility is revealed by the penning of the same letter in a number of different styles. The medium pressure of the writing is a sign of his vitality and a liking for people; he is neither pushy nor retiring but his presence cannot be ignored. The mainly upright writing means control, and the undeviating impulse that flows the letters to the right points to his reaching out to others — two features which show that we have a man who needs companionship and yet is quite capable of enjoying his own company.

PORTRAIT

Willie Rushton is a highly discerning individual in matters of differentiation, capable of subtle distinctions in his reaction to both the abstract and the practical. There is aestheticism, artistic interest and ability, good taste and a sense of proportion which makes him considerate of others and sincere in his approach to all things. He is mentally very active, his mind the major driving force in his life, and not only is he a quick thinker but his fertile imagination produces clever combinations of thought enabling him to link matters of everyday life with his intellectuality so that he is able to take the initiative with his ideas and carry them through to the conclusion he desires.

The thinking is original and efficient so that he is adaptable in his work, his social life and his circumstances in general, but he is primarily concerned with expressing himself freely and fluently and he is pretty inconsiderate towards anything or anyone that does not specifically further that end. Being basically intellectual in outlook, he likes to keep the underlying sensitivity under control, and generally he succeeds in overcoming what is essentially a reserved disposition. His adaptation is not spontaneous; rather it is of a forced type, like that of a man who is not living his life in exactly the way he would like nor indeed the way his true talents dictate. There is, therefore, some moodiness and irritability when his inherent excitability becomes strong enough to disturb his self-control. Certainly, he has developed an independence from his impressionable nature, and this enables him to demonstrate a good degree of purpose in his life. He is devoted to saving both time and unnecessary effort in his dealings with others, and to achieve this he has developed a directnesss of action and a capacity to plunge into the midst of things without preliminaries.

Form and deportment, both social and aesthetic, are important to him, and there is a dislike of affectation and superficiality in whatever guise. Reflective and speculative, he experiences conflict between his self-protective and his self-expressive urges, so that he tends to scale the intellectual heights as well as plumb the materialistic and instinctive depths of his nature. This adds further to the continual activity in which he indulges, brought about by unstilled ambition and dissatisfaction with that he has so far achieved.

There is no real discord between his private and public life, neither being sacrificed upon the altar of the other, but he does tend to suppress feelings in favour of his occupation, which probably receives the bulk of his interest and attention.

To summarize the personality of Willie Rushton: he is the possessor of a sensitive, mercurial mind which is nevertheless orderly and cautious; he is able to think in the abstract and to arrange matters critically; he can progress from intellectual heights to materialistic depths, and there is within him an urge for continuous activity. He is not, however, exorbitant or exaggerated in his aspirations, and there would be no bitterness should he fail to achieve a goal. He has come to terms with himself and with reality, and finds much satisfaction in his life.

The sensitive, artistic temperament is usually composed of conflict and uncertainty, and it is this mobility of mind — the result of these conflicts — which is the hallmark of a truly original personality.

'A pretty fair assessment' — Willie Rushton

Jonathan Dimbleby

Dear Mr Holmes,

Thank you for your letter. This is my handwritten response!

You are at liberty to diagnose it - if you can read it - as you will. I would be glad of a sight of your conclusions before publication.

Best wishes

Jonathan Dimbleby.

HANDWRITING HIGHLIGHTS

The writing is decipherable but not legible, and we can see from this that he is a man who is unable to compromise easily with the world if it would cost him his originality. The construction of both letters and words is quite relaxed, which indicates that he is rather easygoing and has a liking for unusual, rather than mundane, tasks. Look carefully at the letters 'd' and see how the tops of the strokes curl back to the left. This feature appears in the writing of poets from many nations and reveals their reflective nature. The slant to the right speaks of his liking for people, but the uneven pressure pattern states that he can lose his temper with them. Many of the letters are cleverly simplified and contracted, and there are few if any superfluous strokes. This aspect of handwriting indicates a fine intellect and the ability to get to the heart of the matter without wasting too much time on the non-essentials. Hooks at the beginning and end of many strokes reveal the nervous energy present; an over-taxing of this energy could lead to an inability to relax.

PORTRAIT

Here is a man who guards his originality, who will not accept praise at face value if he fears that it might damage the image he has of himself, a rebellious figure who does not adapt easily to the demands of those around him. His ideas are bright and spontaneous, and he likes to present them with an air of individuality. He has a marked preference for going his own way and not being tied down by bureaucracy and red tape. His style is easygoing and somewhat nonconformist; he does not like a by-the-book approach and neither is he overfond of repetitive tasks, while he responds well to a challenge. Somewhat unpredictable, he prefers to do things on the spur of the moment, and he can show a quick up-and-down flare of temper with little warning, but all is forgiven and forgotten a short time later.

He is a sociable man, with a love of life, who inclines strongly towards the outside world, and he has an acute social awareness. He enjoys meeting people and sharing with them his feelings, indeed, his main interests are focused on people and their behaviour, and it is through the stimulation he gets from his contact with them that he values his own worth.

His cultural and literary interests give him scope for his original enterprise which he exercises efficiently and enthusiastically.

His mind is reflective and philosophical, with great receptivity to abstract influences. He has fine powers of concentration and intellectual penetration, making his thoughts rational and clear; yet although there is a desire to think carefully, his thoughts will sometimes follow each other with such rapidity that he will not have the time to organize them properly and to present them lucidly.

Sometimes he will silence his emotions, and this inhibition of expression will bring on periods of moodiness and irritability. Usually he appears self-possessed and this is helped along by a strong, conscious self-control. Goal-minded and with a strong sense of purpose, he has a straightforward approach to matters and does not waste his time on non-essentials. He is cool and matter-of-fact; a mature realist who is extremely business-minded. He has a restless energy which tends to make him impulsive, although he has managed to curb this trait successfully.

He is an unaffected man with a naturally friendly disposition that contains a balancing control of firmness. Jonathan Dimbleby has also managed to keep a balanced relationship between his private and professional lives, but, perhaps more important, he has managed to channel all his creative talents to useful purpose and thereby satisfy his desire for achievement.

'I read your revelations about my personality with great curiosity. It certainly seems to fit' — Jonathan Dimbleby

Derek Nimmo

1st August 1st

Dear Mr. Holmes

I am sorry to have been so long in replying to your letter of May 13th but I have been in hospital undergoing a heart by-pass operation. I am right handed.

Yours sincerely

Derek Nimmo

Nimmo

HANDWRITING HIGHLIGHTS

Short strokes at the end of the last letter of many words point to abruptness and self-control. The suppression of personal feelings for the sake of formality is shown by the firmly drawn arches or arcades that make up the letters 'm' 'n' and 'h'.

Isolated letter forms show the intuitiveness present, and the rhythmic, irregular writing is a clear sign that the inherent excitability of his temperament is well controlled and creatively directed. Nervous energy as well as the inability to relax is evidenced by the hooks that appear throughout, especially at the end of strokes. Simplification of letter-form tells of his high intelligence, and the way in which he seems to have created his own letter styles makes it clear that he likes to go his own way and do his own thing. Intellectualism and soaring upper zone strokes go together, as do leanness in the middle zone and matter-of-factness. Good spacing between words and between lines clearly shows that he is a good speaker and stylist.

PORTRAIT

There is nothing so important to Derek Nimmo as being able to express his ideas freely and fluently, and he is pretty inconsiderate towards anything or anybody that does not specifically cater for this requirement. There is not the slightest desire on his part to compromise his originality in any way as this particular aspect of his personality is of much importance to him. He is truly idealistic, and his agile mind is speculating constantly about matters which affect him. The fount of all this activity is the need to make his dreams a reality; there is also considerable nervous energy and enthusiasm arising from his fertile imagination, and these features colour all his activities. About him is a sureness of purpose and when he moves towards his goal he concentrates on its needs and requirements to the exclusion of all else. It can now be seen that even though his temperament is inherently excitable he has nevertheless managed to exert a good measure of control and creative direction.

He is rather conventional, which makes him cautious and conformist in both dress and behaviour, and he is a worrier who likes to feel that he is in control of his working environment as well as matters in general. It is safe to assume, therefore, that once he has accepted any kind of responsibility for the actions of others, he tends to be rather excessive in his supervision of them and to interfere unduly with the way in which they carry out their appointed tasks. These are the hallmarks of the perfectionist.

He is not a moody man, but when his control lets him down he can display a strong outburst of anger and frustration. His deepest feelings are kept hidden, making his reactions difficult to assess. He has adapted well to the demands made upon him by his profession, but the adaptation has not been easy as he has had to straightjacket his personal emotions and feelings for the sake of the formality which he considers so important. Questions with an emotional content embarrass him and to compensate for this discomfort he will respond in a flippant and light-hearted manner.

He is a headstrong and wilful man who can at times be very opinionated, and this makes it extremely difficult for some people to deal effectively with him. His formal nature also makes him somewhat stiff and inflexible, and he is, therefore, usually either strongly for or against some particular principle. With his straightforward approach, he can be abrupt and he is able to plunge into the middle of a task without wasting time on irrelevant preliminaries. He is able to take the initiative and not only does he dream up ideas but he also sees them through to a satisfactory conclusion as well.

Although his need for people is paramount to him, the majority of those he knows are rather superficial acquaintances. His really close friends are few in number, but with these he will work hard at developing the relationship. Undoubtedly his instinctive feelings and idealistic dreams influence him more than the demands of social contact.

There is a restless energy and an underlying excitability which, up to a point, makes him dependent upon the approval and the plaudits of others. He is driven by a wish to make the most of his talents, and can be carried away quite easily by his enthusiastic nature. He does have some difficulty in spanning the gap between his ambition and the extent to which he is prepared to go to fulfil that ambition, as he will only go all-out for that which he believes he can achieve. He is cautious and self-involved to the point where his doubts about his capabilities prevent the full development of his talent, but for all that he lives his life in a way that gives him much satisfaction and enables him to have a genuine pride in his achievements.

I suppose one could say that he is a bit eccentric; and one could certainly say that he is quite capable of making mountains out of molehills. Honest in his endeavours, he abhors affectation and superficiality, and will go to any lengths to avoid those who are so afflicted.

Derek Nimmo puts on the same face in private that he wears in public, but there is another side to him that is rarely seen, and maybe, just maybe, some of that has been revealed in this profile.

'Jolly accurate . . . well done' — Derek Nimmo

George Cole

Dear Mr. Holman.

                I hope you are
not going to tell me I
have no artistic tendencies.
I'd hate to give up
acting after all these
years.

              Yours sincerely.

              George Cole

Right Handed.

HANDWRITING HIGHLIGHTS

Light pressure indicates great mobility of character, and the isolated letter-forms speak strongly of intuitiveness. The letter-forms also show considerable deviations from those taught at school, indicating the originality and creativity that is so much a part of this personality. The darting staccato strokes mirror his impulsiveness, and the rising base line of the writing reveal the optimistic side of his nature. Hooks at the beginning and end of many strokes show that nervous energy is present, and the rising signature clearly indicates that he feels more than confident in his ability to cope with the majority of his problems. Wide spacing between words speaks of his capacity for clear thought, while the way in which he drops his capital letters below the writing line is a sign that he has a real understanding of what it is that makes people tick. The way some letters level down to an almost straight line clearly illustrates that he has a shrewd and diplomatic mind, and whilst George Cole is ethically beyond suspicion it would seem that he has many of the attributes of the characters he portrays.

PORTRAIT

The sensitive staccato writing of George Cole clearly reveals his intuitive nature and great mobility of expression. He is a creative personality who pays scant regard to convention, and when the occasion demands, he can change his character shape and become what is expected of him.

He tends to keep himself to himself, preferring the company of known, close associates to more superficial relationships. It is essential that he lets his active mind have full rein as imagination and external impressions have a great effect upon him.

His working speed is quick, even and reliable, and he is purposeful in his general approach. Rarely is he disturbed by his impulses, and yet he does not blindly impose controls on himself and follow set rules as this would make him rigid, clumsy and constrained. There are good powers of observation and concentration, and these are combined with rapid thought processes, objectivity and a good critical sense. Hardly surprising then that he has a strong desire to express his particularity and further develop and broaden his scope.

He has an independent outlook and a calm, self-reliant nature, and appears, to those who know him well, to be rather clinical in his relationships. He fears that getting too close to those he does not know well might compromise him or make him lose part of his identity. This slight aloofness also enables him to ensure clear and reasoned thought and as he can be unduly impressed by the views and criticisms of others it is important for him to make this conscious effort. He is the possessor of a logical and adjustable attitude, and approaches situations in a straightforward way. He likes new ideas and situations and he is not too enthusiastic about routine, although being rather easygoing he will tolerate it if he must.

His impulsiveness has, on occasions, made it seem as if he works on the principle of 'act now, pay later'. In his life he unerringly knows that which is important and that which is not and he well realizes how the parts of a given situation fit the whole, which gives him the capacity to expound intelligently on a wide range of subjects.

He wishes to be understood by others and will go to great lengths to achieve this, having no inhibitions to bar his natural drive for self-expression and communication. Broadminded, tolerant and quite generous, his attitude towards others is one of frankness and friendliness, and he likes to oblige where he can. He can be changeable in his approach to matters, at times showing unconstraint and dash and at other times displaying reserve and caution.

He has an abundance of nervous energy and he finds if difficult to stay still for long. There is an infectious enthusiasm which permeates through to everyone around him, but like most people who have reserves of nervous energy he becomes listless when he depletes those reserves and this can lead to insomnia and loss of appetite.

There is great clarity of thought, but sometimes he takes a delight in being obscure and can take an equal delight in, and refuge behind, ambiguity.

With the awareness that comes from his intuitiveness, he is able to show tact and diplomacy in his dealings with others, and this makes him a shrewd and businesslike person, well able to look after his affairs. If it will make you happy, he will show you what you want to see and he does this with great skill, kindness and understanding. His adaptation is that of the chameleon, carried out with subtlety and finesse; he could not have chosen a better career than that of the actor — the man who lives through someone else.

'I'm fascinated and delighted with myself' — George Cole

Auberon Waugh

Dear Mr Holmes,

here is a specimen of my handwriting
– rather self conscious on this occasion, I fear. I
am right-handed. It is not normally quite
so spidery as this.

I hope you will take _Literary Review_,
obtainable from 51 Beak St W1 for £14 pa

Yours sincerely
Auberon Waugh

HANDWRITING HIGHLIGHTS

Although the script is illegible, it is nevertheless of a good
standard and many of the letters appear to be part of some
private alphabet. From this one may deduce that this is an
awkward man who has no desire whatsoever to compromise with the world at the cost of his originality. The way
in which he simplifies many of the letters indicates that
he can easily separate that which is important from that
which is not. There is great originality, irregularity and
lack of discipline within the writing, pointing to a very
original but somewhat off-balance personality. There are

conflicting slants to the letters in the middle zone, which indicate strong conflicts in his social life, and a form of social adolescence that gives rise to difficulties of relationship and adjustment. The letters 'n' 'm' and 'h' are formed by using a vault-like stroke called an arcade and this means he has adapted to the world without revealing his inner self. It also means that tradition and convention both play an important part in his life. The pressure is light although there are some heavier patterns which reveal an elastic mind that is uneven in temper.

PORTRAIT

The personality of Auberon Waugh is so complex that it is extremely difficult to choose a starting point. The obvious suggestion — start at the beginning — is rather meaningless as there is no clearly defined beginning or end to the workings of this mercurial mind. Perhaps the most strongly indicated features are those of intelligence and imagination, which appear in virtually every facet of the script. Culture and literacy are also characteristic of this speculative and reflective man; he will not compromise if that compromise is at the cost of his originality, and one of his main concerns is that he should be able to express his ideas freely and fluently; as a result he is not interested in anything which does not specifically serve his purpose. This can make him inconsiderate of the wishes of others.

He has firm convictions, strong prejudices, and violent likes and dislikes; the resultant streak of obstinacy means that he does not court popularity for its own sake. There is a virtually complete lack of regard for whether he is understood as rarely does he think that others can be right in their opinions. The unfamiliar holds a challenge for him, and there is a real liking for change and innovation so he is best suited to projects requiring creativity and imagination. This great originality exacts the price of a somewhat out-of-balance personality who refuses to adapt to society and who rebels against conformity.

There is little emotional contact with the outside world, and personal questions are answered with reticence. This difficulty in displaying his feelings stems from the fact that he tends not to feel close to people, although he can put on a show of friendliness when necessary, without revealing his inner thoughts. Self-interest can make him appear detached at times but in reality his discerning mind is continually taking in what is going on. He has a strong feeling towards the outside world, and as the fantasy forces of his mind have been intellectualized there is a deep understanding of people, towards whom he displays a courtesy of a disinterested sort, seeing through those with whom he is dealing and reacting accordingly. Invariably he knows when he has made his point, going just so far and then stopping.

The emotions are quick-changing, as is the hand that guides the pen, but overall he exercises good control and the mind takes over whenever important decisions have to be made, so that he displays at such time a cool matter-of-factness and a business-minded realism.

He is a difficult man to understand and an equally difficult man to please, and being rather modest by nature he abhors affectation and superficiality, preferring instead straightforward relationships in both his professional and private lives. Rather than emphatic gestures, he is able finely to judge his capabilities so as not to strive for that which is outside his compass. There are social aspirations, and form and deportment are stressed by him both socially and aesthetically. The factors in his life which he considers important are descent, tradition, convention and manners, and he has high regard for well-regulated social relations.

There are conflicts within him regarding his social life, and he tends to swing between periods of withdrawn solitude and of excited sociability. This form of social adolescence has given rise to the difficulties of relation-ship and adjustment.

There is a lack of consistent drive, as whilst it can be strong at times there does appear to be the occasional loss of purpose. Not always even-tempered, he can give a dramatic moment emotional emphasis, a trait which strongly indicates a quarrelsome and litigious tendency.

His basic nervousness is, however, disciplined by his being actively engrossed in his work, and his constant awareness of purpose and direction means that he can quite adequately sustain both thought and action towards a goal.

Often critical, always creative, Auberon Waugh has managed to come to terms with his turbulent tempera-ment. There are no pretensions — what you see is what he is, both in private and in public, and neither life is given prominence over the other. In many ways this is a contradictory personality, being both desirous of and yet rebelling against form but whichever aspect gains, albeit for a short time, the upper hand, overall the personality is vital, full of interest and never, ever, boring.

'I'm delighted with nearly everything you write about me'
— Auberon Waugh

Sam Wanamaker

Dear Mr. Holmes –
Thank you for
your letter and request
for a sample of my
handwriting. Here it is.
I am right handed.
Very sincerely
Sam Wanamaker

HANDWRITING HIGHLIGHTS

A somewhat illegible script containing many well simplified letters clearly points to an irreverent nature, and
the many hooks scattered throughout indicate nervous
energy and enthusiasm. This man will not sacrifice his
originality — a trait shown by the highly individual way
in which he shapes and joins his letters — and the soaring
upper zones are a sign of his idealism. There is fluency in

the flow of his script from left to right, while the letters have a distinct slant to the right, a feature representing his need for people; the way in which the letters of some words taper to a near-straight line shows that he is, however, shrewd and diplomatic with a toughness of character that will let him take advantage of others in order to achieve his aim.

He has many different ways of forming the same letter which means that he is extremely versatile, and his vitality is shown by the medium pressure with which he applies pen to paper.

PORTRAIT

The handwriting of Sam Wanamaker clearly indicates that he is a rather irreverent man who disregards form and convention in order better to express his creativity. He demands freedom of expression for a mind that is brimming with energy and liveliness, and there is a considerable store of nervous energy that makes him tense and enthusiastic. He will only undertake a task if it fits in with his conception of originality as he is not interested in popular acclaim for its own sake. His personality comes over from the script as being highly original yet slightly out of focus, making it hardly surprising that he finds difficulty in adapting to the prescribed norm.

He loves undertakings that require him to use his creativity and imagination and compel him to enter an arena that is alien and strange. He is also an impulsive man and is quite capable of saying and doing things which later might give him cause for regret. He is able to express his emotions easily, and will from time to time fluctuate between the states of elation and despair. The mind speculates on projects for the future, ideas forming and developing in a logical way so that they are usually practical.

He has a friendly, adaptable nature, and is sensitive to

external impressions although he does try to control the amount of influence they exert over him. His outlook on life has a certain inconsistency about it as he will, for instance, examine a situation in detail at one moment only to generalize about it a short time later. His idealistic dreams influence him much more than does any desire for prestige or fame.

There is much initiative and élan in the make-up as well as impatience and periodic lapses in concentration. There is some lack of assurance at times of critical decision-making, but the uncertainty is not allowed to stand in the way of his progress. He is a good talker and entertainer with a strong desire to communicate with others but he cannot always be sufficiently concerned to make the effort. His ideas are good and his perception sound and relevant with the inherent excitability of his temperament being generally well controlled and creatively directed. He needs room to manipulate and to breathe, and there is an extravagance of feeling which can lead to his aesthetic sense overpowering his caution.

There is a need to be with people and this need finds fulfilment through his self-confident sociability. His attitude towards others is normally one of frankness and friendliness and he likes to oblige where he can, but as he is pretty tough, shrewd and diplomatic, he finds it difficult not to take advantage of others in order to achieve his aim. In the main he sees only black and white and rarely if ever does he allow himself the luxury of a comfortable vagueness in his dealings, either with others or with situations. Sam Wanamaker is a man who has the ability to make full and purposeful use of all his qualities in the pursuit of his aims, and this is one of the main prerequisites of success in any field.

Jilly Cooper

Dear Mr Holmes,

Thank you for your letter. Last time a graphologist wrote to ask me for a sample of my writing, I copied a bit of Oscar Wilde, and they said I must be literate because my punctuation was so good. This time I'm not cheating.

Yours sincerely

Jilly Cooper

JILLY COOPER

HANDWRITING HIGHLIGHTS

The capital letters 'I' are straight and without flourishes,
showing that she gets down to things in a straightforward

manner, and this quality is also indicated by the lack
of starting, or lead-in, strokes to the first letters of the
majority of words. Each time she writes the same letter
it takes on a different form, and there is no doubt that she
appears to have invented her own alphabet. This means
that there is a surfeit of originality and creativity within
the personality.

In many words the letters taper — starting large at the
beginning of the word and becoming smaller towards
the end. This quality is usually displayed by tactful and
diplomatic people and those with shrewd, calculating
minds. The tension of the strokes in their left-to-right
progression is quite strong, and yet there are some areas
of weakness, pointing to her good sense of purpose which
only occasionally lets her down.

The varying size of the middle zone states that she views
life with some inconsistency, generalizing about a subject
one day and examining it in detail the next.

PORTRAIT

The mind of Jilly Cooper is fired by vision and imagination, and there is a very real need for her to express her
ideas in an individual way and constantly to develop her
own particular style of doing things. Quite often she finds
herself out of step with society, and this is due to her
disregard of form and convention. Although the mind is
sharp and discerning and well able to grasp the essentials
of a subject quickly, there is nevertheless an emotionalism underlying the intellect which causes conflict and
leads to a continual craving for change and innovation.
There are times when she is driven by a longing to make
something more of her dreams, stemming from unstilled
ambition and a rather vague dissatisfaction.

Considerable nervous energy and an inner enthusiasm
that have their origins in her imagination together make

nervous demands upon her that force her into continuous activity, making it extremely difficult for her to relax. The mind is not too well disciplined, which means that she can swing from a down-to-earth and realistic approach to unrest and, even, a lack of coherent thought; the intellect usually wins, however, and balance is restored. Self-contained and rather aloof, she is nevertheless generally friendly and certainly possesses charm but she does not permit a ready intimacy and has difficulty in revealing her deepest feelings. Her adaptation to the world about her is like that of a chameleon, enabling her to avoid conforming rigidly to any particular code of behaviour, and this is essential to someone who resents restriction and restraint being placed upon the freedom of thought and action which she considers so essential to her effective functioning.

She is confident and at her best when working on her own, or where she has personal rather than shared authority, but if she has to consult with others she loses much of her firmness and becomes rather ill at ease.

Her spirit is competitive, and although she does rather coast along on the tide of circumstance, she invariably manages to ensure that her individual expression is not lost nor her essential purpose sacrificed to laziness. While her headstrongness makes her difficult to deal with it also makes her reliable and thorough so long as her interest in a project can be maintained. She is a person with convictions and she is willing to fight for her beliefs, the strongest of which is the belief in herself.

In brief, that which has so far been found in the handwriting of Jilly Cooper shows us that she is fascinated by new ideas, the unusual and the unfamiliar; that routine is irksome to her as she is ideally suited to situations requiring a surfeit of creativity so that she need not concern herself with too many small points of detail. She can be impulsive, saying and doing things on the spur of the moment which later might give her cause for regret.

Surely any person with a mind as active, fertile and full
of ideas as this must have connections with 'Tir nan Og'
— Land of the ever young.

*'Your assessment seems remarkably accurate to me. In fact
appallingly accurate. My husband thought so too'* — Jilly
Cooper

Robert Robinson

Dear Mr Holmes —
  I was seduced by a
typewriter at an early
age, thus my hand-
writing remains a child-
ish scrawl !
        Yours sincerely
        Robert Robinson

HANDWRITING HIGHLIGHTS

A careful examination of all the letters reveal small hooks
at the beginning of many strokes which certainly points
to the writer having an abundance of nervous energy,
and from which we can also deduce that he is tense,

talkative and very enthusiastic. The layout in general is a
bit untidy and this demonstrates that he has little time for
appearance for its own sake and that he puts his efforts
directly into the many projects he has still to accomplish.
The writing is relaxed and free flowing, reflecting his liking for new ideas and situations where he has to use his
creative talents. Strong pressure shows that he has strong
emotions, but the upright nature of the letters tells us that
he is able to control these emotions quite well. The letters
'n' and 'm' are produced with wavy lines and from this we
may gather that kindness and tolerance are strong in him,
and that they will combine to produce the characteristic
role of mediator for which he is so well known. The letters
are joined together in a way that indicates a logical formation of ideas in his mind, and the signature is identical to
the rest of the script, meaning that he is without pretension. The writing is surprisingly undisciplined for a man
who appears to be so tightly controlled, and this shows
just how strong is the force of his will.

PORTRAIT

Tense, very enthusiastic and talkative, best sums up the
man we know as Robert Robinson. He is never happier
than when he is expressing his bright and original ideas in
his own individual way, and he displays impatience and
irritability if he feels that his personal enterprise is threatened. His mind is independent and alert, enabling him to
think in a systematic and purposeful manner so that he
can appraise everyday events realistically and assess the
potential of a given situation. He is a calculating, rational
man with the ability to think in the abstract and he does
not find it at all difficult to take an idea and see the many
possibilities contained therein.

Whilst he enjoys a rich emotional life, his emotions are
expressed in a controlled and positive manner, although

he will on occasion display moodiness and temper, as beneath the air of self-confidence and calm there is some strain and tension; overall, however, the head strongly rules the heart.

He enjoys a natural relationship with the surrounding world, and is an obliging character, open to influence, and capable of being impressed by another person's viewpoint. He is a mediator, preferring to take the smooth way and trying, where possible, to avoid unnecessary conflict, a natural pourer of oil on troubled waters.

There is good order in his life but he can irritate himself with feelings of uncertainty, particularly when he tries too much to live up to his preconceived idea of himself. Although he does appear rather self-contained and somewhat aloof, and experiences some difficulty in revealing his innermost feelings, he is nevertheless a friendly person and possesses much charm. He has a highly developed critical sense which can, however, make him appear detached and lacking in emotional response.

There is tenacity, and a good determinate purpose, while the behaviour is spontaneous and forthright, showing us a man who will defend his principles strongly. Mature and unassuming, he concentrates his attention chiefly upon the realities of everyday life, and his practical outlook makes him particularly well balanced.

There is a fully justified pride in his achievements, and he holds himself in good esteem, not thinking that he should hold his head either higher or lower than anyone else. Being preoccupied with the present, he rarely daydreams and tends to take things as they come, and as he is a person of energy he pursues his aims vigorously, and usually to a conclusion which he deems satisfactory.

To sum up, Robert Robinson is a man of intelligence with a clever combination of thoughts, and whose head, in spite of the underlying emotionality, definitely rules his heart. Independent, cool and self-confident, he leans towards order and method. For all the adjustments he has made to his life, his main difficulties are still unresolved and he is often disturbed by unexpressed yearnings, clearly showing that he still has things to do and places to go.

Although he is inclined to extroversion, likes attractive clothes, and has a desire for an interesting social life, he behaves naturally and unpretentiously in public as in private, neither life being given too much prominence over the other.

The definition, in science, of the word 'catalysis' is: the effect produced by a substance that, without undergoing change, aids a chemical change in other substances. Robert Robinson has a catalytic effect upon others, in that without undergoing change himself he induces a profound change in those around him.

'Certainly!' — Robert Robinson

Keith Waterhouse

Dear Mr Holmes

I hope this page of notes will serve your purpose. I'm right handed.

Yours

Keith Waterhouse

HANDWRITING HIGHLIGHTS

Some of the letters 't' have not been crossed and none of the letters 'i' have been dotted. Normally this would be attributed to carelessness, but in this handwriting it reveals independence, as high intelligence is revealed in the superb simplification of many of the letter forms. There is some neglect and carelessness, but this is due to the thoughts of the writer outstripping his pen. Distinctiveness and individuality are shown in the way he pens his signature, the forename and surname joined in one continuous movement. Legibility is quite poor and yet, as stated earlier, the writing is indicative of good intelligence, therefore we read into this combination that he is not particularly concerned about the opinions of others. The easy flow of the writing shows quite positively that he needs freedom to express his thoughts and actions, and it also depicts his liking for tasks which use to the full his creative abilities. This is exuberant writing, displaying initiative and élan as well as impatience. This last, rather negative, characteristic can be seen quite clearly in the lack of careful finish to many letters and words.

PORTRAIT

Independence is probably the most outstanding feature of this highly creative, cheerful and resilient individual. He is not particularly concerned about the opinions of others, although he will never ignore constructive advice and criticism. He has an active approach to all things connected with his work in particular and his life in general, and he is not at all fearful of the future or of his ability to cope. Self-sufficient and resourceful, he seldom broods on past mistakes or missed opportunities, preferring to make his own decisions, right or wrong, and then stand by their outcome. He is not a joiner of groups or movements, and indeed he is often critical of group standards and as a result can suffer loneliness. He prefers to extract himself from any difficult situation in which he might find himself without asking for help from others and he prefers to be alone at times of emotional stress.

His personality is highly original, although a shade off-centre in the sense that he does not adapt too easily to the demands of society and tends to rebel against orthodoxy and conformity. His ideas are bright and original, and they are expressed using his own brand of individuality so that he objects strongly to having petty restrictions imposed upon his creativity, becoming irritable and impatient. Normally, however, he is easygoing. He loves new ideas and unusual situations, and finds routine for its own sake irksome, although when necessary he is able to exert a discipline on his working environment.

He is far more at home with projects which require the use of imagination and creativity, and this can lead to him being impulsive so that he blurts things out with little thought for the consequences. He is also subject to some contradictory tendencies, being at one time sociable and pulled towards the world, whilst at another time he will be reserved and rather introspective.

He displays initiative and élan in the way he approaches his work, but he can also exhibit signs of impatience and lack of concentration due to his sensitivity, which result in an uncertainty that gives him great mobility in his approach. This means that he can make progress as he is able to change both his attitude and his mind when he is suitably impressed by the views and opinions of another.

The never-resting mind does not consider itself bound too tightly by acquired forms and traditions, and he tries to steer clear of conventionality: in his case this has lead to some novel and unique achievements. Imagination and outside impressions influence him greatly, and his impulses and emotions are too strong to be easily muzzled by self-discipline. He certainly feels strongly about his ideas, which can make him argumentative as he needs freedom to express them without undue restraint. The thoughts are rational and he is clearsighted, quickly recognizing how events interrelate. The thought processes are very rapid and fluent, and with his intelligence he is well able to put his ideas into effect. His powers of observation are good, as is his ability to concentrate on whatever is the current project. Being mentally very active and having a highly developed imagination, he does occasionally find himself in an emotional stew about something or other, and at such times his judgements can be coloured by the turmoil.

Although generally shrewd, discreet and diplomatic, there are times when he can throw caution to the winds and become uncompromising and obstinate in the defence of his views; then you would see the quick up-and-down flare of temper of which he is capable.

He is a lively person who is dominantly positive although there are a few weak spots. He has, for example, a tendency to reflect just a little too much on the past and this can give rise to misgivings which tend to inhibit the free and full development of his natural and genuine expression.

His mind is so full of ideas and there is so much creative imagination that, to borrow a phrase from Kipling, he fills 'the unforgiving minute with sixty seconds' worth of distance run'.

'My nearest and dearest agree with me that your reading is so perceptive and accurate. . . . How do you do it?' — Keith Waterhouse

Purpose

Those who have a strong sense of purpose are usually those who exercise great control over themselves and their activities through the strength of their will. This reveals itself in script that is even in size and extremely well laid out, testifying to the ability to exert a continuous control over writing movements. The strokes that join the letters together have a strong tension, and the writing always seems to be in a hurry to reach the right-hand side of the page.

Ralph Hammond Innes, CBE

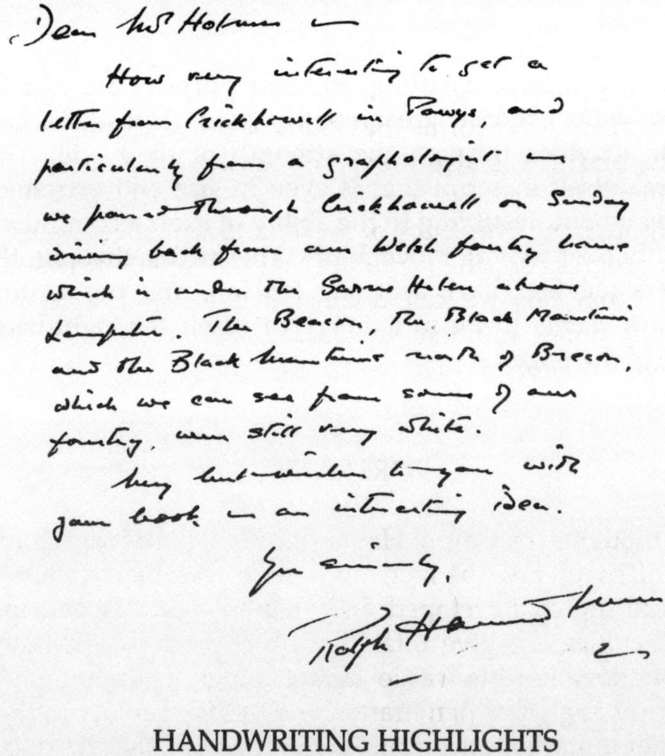

[handwritten letter]

Dear Mr Holmes —

How very interesting to get a letter from Crickhowell in Powys, and particularly from a graphologist — we passed through Crickhowell on Sunday driving back from our Welsh fishing house which is under the Sawdde Helen above Llangadog. The Beacon, The Black Mountain and the Black Mountains north of Brecon, which we can see from some of our fishing, were still very white.

Many thanks indeed to you with your book — an interesting idea.

Yours sincerely,

Ralph Hammond Innes

HANDWRITING HIGHLIGHTS

Small writing of a good standard that is also well laid out and presented indicates that the mind of the writer is quick and that his approach to matters in general is just as orderly. The continuous control over the writing movements can only come from someone with a great strength of will, and, as simplification of letters is diverse, from someone with a high level of intelligence. The rightward slant of the writing clearly shows his interest in and liking for people, and the way in which he has different ways of producing the same letter speaks strongly of creativity. Some letters stand apart from their fellows whilst others are connected in a long flow, which means that he can solve problems both by logic and intuition. A truly formidable combination.

High bars to the letters 't' are also strong, pointing to a questing mind that is not easily influenced and is able to think in a purposeful manner. Again, creativity is shown by the many letter forms that dwindle down to a tapering stroke, and this is also the sign of a shrewd and tactical diplomat.

Although the main body of the writing is quite horizontal in its progression, the signature takes a definite upwards path. From this we can deduce that Ralph Hammond Innes is quite confident in his ability to cope with the problems of life.

PORTRAIT

The thoughts of Ralph Hammond Innes are sagacious and often in the abstract, and his intellectual resource is more highly developed and trained than his perceptive faculties. To give total free play to his imagination is not altogether his way of doing things, his preference being for analytical penetration and getting rapidly to the heart of a matter, and from this we can see that he does not care for exaggerated expression and style, favouring simple, rational and concise methods of conveying what he has to say.

As well as having a quick mind and an orderly approach, he is a good organizer, and when these qualities are combined with his disciplined imagination, it results in ideas that are realistic and practical. There is also a great strength of will that enables him to exert strong control over his feelings and impulses, meaning that he can regulate the energies of his mind. He gets to grips with the essentials of a subject very quickly, and progresses through logical ideas step by step to a satisfactory conclusion. The level of intelligence is really quite remarkable and the thought processes are very fast, so that he will avoid at any cost restrictions being placed upon his questing mind, as he needs freedom and space for his thoughts and acts.

He is unusually unprejudiced, impartial and objective in his attitude towards people and events, and with his reflective and speculative mind this makes him extremely interested in the world at large. He is the creative type who does not consider himself bound too tightly by the customary conventions of life, and he chooses his own way regardless of how others might react. He is, in addition, a practical psychologist, instinctively understanding what it is that makes people tick, and when he has to deal with others he adapts himself easily, demonstrating that he is both a tactician and a shrewd diplomat. He is both alert and capable when negotiating with others, and always ready to adopt a new line of attack or defence, while avoiding getting himself pinned down.

Indicated strongly is the fact that he will put work before friendship, and creative satisfaction before leisure. He also comes across as an authoritarian figure with a strong desire to control events, but there is a personal modesty about him and the affection he has for his subject is plain, as is the way his mind covers the entire field of his art and masters all its detail.

Spontaneous and quick reacting, he works with zest and élan, but he can be somewhat careless and overhasty, and show a level of impatience and irritation towards people whose reactions are slower than his. Occasionally, he allows into his mind many more impressions than he can easily assimilate, and at such times his judgement becomes blurred as to what is important and what is not. Part of this difficulty is caused by his not always pausing in his relation with the outside world, on those occasions being compelled more by impulse than guided by reason and consideration. When the impulses are controlled, the thoughts follow a sequence or pattern of ideas, and he is able quickly to disassemble the constituents of a complex situation and then discern the place for each part, thereby directing his creative thinking to constructive effect. He can also concentrate upon changing and varied spheres of work, switching from one idea or task to another with ease. Although determined, and even compulsive, he adapts his attitude to changed circumstances, and the fact that he has not adopted a definite and fixed point of view about most things gives him great flexibility of thought and does not narrow him down to specific groups of fixed principles. Where he does hold views and convictions, they are strong; and he tends to see mainly black and white, refusing to compromise with any of the many shades of grey.

He is a wilful man and this can make him difficult to deal with at times. He is also a man of honour and principle, a bit stiff and inflexible, but you can trust him implicitly and rely upon him to do a job well and to the best of his ability. He is young at heart and will always remain so.

It is easy, by the use of graphology, to take the lid off a character and to examine it as if it were a pocket watch. You can see the component parts and it is even possible to examine their interrelationships one with the other, but with a personality such as the one belonging to Hammond Innes it is impossible to calculate all the impressions and experiences that have gone into producing such a complex movement. I have shown just a little of what makes him tick and that is how it should be.

'I am impressed that you got such a reasonable character study' — Ralph Hammond Innes

Charlie Chester

Dear Derek.

*Although writing is part of my
living — my actual penmanship
leaves much to be desired*

*However if you can analise This
you have my admiration !*

*I am right handed — and in
my right mind !*

Sincerely

HANDWRITING HIGHLIGHTS

The signature is the most striking part of the script and
clearly demonstrates an attempt to attract attention to
himself. This is a type of vanity, but as the general standard of the writing is so high it would be more accurate to
modify the findings to read it as pride in achievement.

Spacing between words and lines is good, and this shows the orderliness of the mind. A reasonable slant to the right indicates that he reaches out to people and enjoys their company. There are angles in what is otherwise a soft and gentle hand, which means that Charlie is friendly but has more than a hint of firmness. Hooks are present throughout, showing that he is a man of considerable nervous energy and with a capacity for hard work. See how the signature as well as the line beneath it rise, as does the word 'sincerely', whilst the rest of the script is horizontal. This undoubtedly shows that the writer has total confidence in his ability to deal with the problems of life and that his confidence in himself is unshakeable.

PORTRAIT

Charlie Chester is a gentle and considerate man, whose personality is sincere and open. There is about him a sense of order, and his outlook and viewpoint on most subjects are well balanced. Ambitious still but not exaggeratedly so, he is honest in his endeavours to achieve something good so that when he meets with disappointment he can accept it without rancour or bitterness. The reason for this is that his sense of duty and his wish for activity are too highly developed to allow him to indulge in surly inactiveness.

Generally, his ideas are practical as he is able to discipline his imagination but the mind is alert and curious about a wide range of subjects. The feelings are also well controlled, so that he is able to think rationally and this brings a realism into his business and financial affairs. He has a good sense of purpose, and is able to transfer his inner assuredness and persistence to whatever is currently engaging his attention. He makes no attempt to avoid problems, dealing with them as they arise, and, being persevering, he will stay with whatever he is doing even if it is not progressing favourably. At times he will procrastinate and dwell for longer than he should on unimportant details before getting to grips with the main essentials of a subject but this is usually no more than a minor drawback.

Firm but friendly, he knows what he wants from life and goes about achieving his aims in a way that allows him to keep his private life under wraps. He is able to take the initiative in new projects, and, as he is an active man and needs an outlet for his energy if he is to maintain his equilibrium, his nervous energy is applied enthusiastically. This forces him into constant activity and makes it difficult for him to relax, his mind pushing him on to achieve his aims, and his nervous ardour colours much of his thinking and activity. He is intuitive, and can make fast assessments of situations, at such times often appearing somewhat vague, while his agile mind is in fact absorbing all that is happening.

He is very interested in the world and what is happening there, and he reaches out to people, enjoys contact with them, and gives freely of himself. There is nevertheless some reserve and a natural modesty; also indicated is vanity . . . well, perhaps not vanity exactly, more a pride in his achievements — and why not? The Charlie Chester Show has been running for a long time, and from what I have gleaned from the handwriting, there is more to come.

'I am amazed at the end product and I must admit it is pretty accurate' — Charlie Chester

Reserve

Small writing, where the height of the middle zone is 2mm or less, always indicates that the person is reserved, and the smaller the writing the greater the reserve. No matter how outgoing such a person might appear it can be quite safely assumed that there is a part of them that is kept private and never revealed even to the closest of companions.

Roy Kinnear

Mary had a little lamb,
It's fleece was white as snow
And everywhere where Mary went,
The lamb was sure to go.

Roy Kinnear

HANDWRITING HIGHLIGHTS

Reserve is strongly indicated here by the small writing, the arched or arcade letters 'n' 'm' and 'h', and the capital letters 'M' that are without central strokes. Culture is evident in the use of the Greek form of 'e' and 'd'. The letters are very close together, and this certainly means that he was a man who did not find it easy to let go, needing to control his environment as much as possible. The words are quite crowded and cramped, which points to him being pushed along by his impulses rather than guided by his reasoning, but the upright nature of the script in general places a control on those emotions. Legibility is not good and this lack of clarity is due to the use of his own letter shapes, clearly depicting a man who went his own way and followed his instincts. His intuitiveness was adequately displayed by the disconnected letters, and the signature being identical in style to the rest of the writing states that Roy Kinnear was a natural and unpretentious man, whatever indications he might have given to the contrary.

PORTRAIT

If I had to attach a label to Roy Kinnear which best described him, it would read 'passive achiever', and if I then had to enlarge on that statement I would say that as he fitted naturally into his chosen role he had little need to strive mightily to achieve his ambitions. How did he make it all look so easy? Before taking a first step in any new venture he would give much thought to what needed to be accomplished; he would then engage in the most detailed preparatory work so that when he came to the project itself the real work was already behind him and success was assured. One further quality that was useful to him was his ability to respond to happenings by way of reason and logic, and, additionally, to retain the facility for perceiving those less obvious influences that lie behind an event and to react correctly to them in an intuitive way without apparent reason or thought.

To be able to express himself in an original way was more important to him than popularity gained at any price, and he had no intention of being compromised in this regard. If he felt confined or restricted and unable properly to express himself then he could increase his demands on those around him to a quite unreasonable extent and become irritated by the merest trifle.

With his idealism and rather high-flying dreams he could find himself unduly affected by outside influences, but he was usually able to control them in a way that led to a satisfactory blending of imagination and intelligence, enabling him to put his vision into effect.

There appears to have been some lack of consideration for others, but as his interest in abstraction was usually greater than his interest in people this should not come as too much of a surprise. There was also a tendency to seek isolation as he was a very private person, this inclination to avoid relationships also arising from the fact that he found it difficult to put his feelings on show. Nevertheless, those feelings were strong and the restraint that he put on them could make him moody and somewhat unpredictable. His cultured mind was meditative, with some reflection on the past, and it would seem that he was rather introspective, even lonely. The thoughts, however, were strikingly concise and efficient, enabling him to get down to the bare bones of a problem with a minimum of fuss. His, then, was the modesty that comes from an able and thoughtful mind that observes life with accuracy and objectivity. There was also a personal discipline, which enabled him to understand himself and cope with the lack of real firmness which was so much a part of his character, a lack of firmness due to his lack of strong ego ambitions, which in turn contributed heavily to the qualities of impartiality and objectivity that he was able to apply towards people and events. In spite of this apparently uncommitted approach, he was nevertheless totally absorbed by his work, where he was constantly learning and where he displayed an abundance of nervous energy.

In summarizing the personality of Roy Kinnear, I would say that his mind was sharp and discerning, although it might not always have appeared so, and he was capable of subtle distinctions in his reactions towards both people and situations. He concentrated mainly upon the realities of his everyday life, and in so doing clearly displayed his inner maturity. He possessed moderation, and the ability to judge himself properly, so that he did not strive after things outside his range. The result was a contentment of mind which he not only enjoyed himself but was able to impart to others. There was ambition, but not of the exaggerated type which might have disturbed his contentment. He was subject to contradictory impulses, at times being sociable and extrovert in his manner and pulled strongly towards the outside world, whilst at other times being introverted and shrinking away from contact with others. Roy Kinnear had discovered just how far he needed to screw down his mercurial mind to avoid frittering away its energies whilst at the same time allowing its creative talents to emerge and escape. The subtlety of his performances show just how finely he was able to judge the requirement.

'I have never been a great believer in graphology but after reading your summary of me as a person, I couldn't have written it better myself' — Roy Kinnear

Arthur Marshall, MBE

I doubt whether you will find my handwriting of much interest as at my advanced age of nearly 76 my hand wobbles rather a lot! However, here is the specimen for which you asked.

Arthur Marshall (right handed).

HANDWRITING HIGHLIGHTS

This handwriting is small and yet in parts it is quite wide, indicating that we had here a reserved but friendly person. The slant of the letters varies from the vertical to being angled to the right, and this clearly shows that he experienced conflict between self-expressive and self-protective urges. Very small though the writing is, it is quite legible, which means that he was a man of honest intent, and as the writing is quite rigid we may conclude that he liked to be firmly in control of events and was, therefore, not a great lover of surprise parties or occasions where things might get out of hand.

The overall height of the writing is small, which reflects his attempt to maintain a harmony of the mind by never venturing beyond his natural limits. The layout is good, indicating that he lived his life to useful purpose, while the signature being no different from the other writing means that his behaviour was natural.

PORTRAIT

Arthur Marshall's reflective and speculative mind was one that worked in a consistent and rational way, making him systematic and purposeful. It was also an orderly mind, enabling him to develop ideas logically, step by step, to a point where he achieved his desire to be understood, as he was fundamentally a sincere and considerate communicator. Used to thinking in the abstract, he could, by critically arranging and connecting matters, take the initiative and carry through whatever he began to a satisfactory conclusion.

Cautious and conformist in his approach, he tended to be a bit of a worrier, who liked to establish as much control as possible over his life. Generally, the temperament was quite even and predictable, although he did tend to bottle up his emotions so that when control was lost, albeit momentarily, there was quite an outburst of temper. He generally exercised control by the simple expedient of turning emotional problems into academic exercises and it is, therefore, understandable why events such as surprise parties were discouraged, as the resulting loss of control could make him embarrassed and uncomfortable.

Occasionally, he would display a wilfulness and obstinacy, and at those times he could be a difficult man to please and understand. His character was upright, and somewhat stiff and inflexible, and he was a man of conviction with strong beliefs — one of which was belief in himself — and he displayed a readiness to defend his convictions.

The mind was young and the personality mature, so that he concentrated upon the realities of his everyday life, striving to achieve and maintain a harmony of the mind by rarely, if ever, attempting to venture beyond his natural capabilities, which kept him disposed to both contentment and happiness.

Arthur Marshall was a natural and unpretentious man in both his public and private lives, indicating an equipoise between the two, with no inclination to assume a different behaviour in either. From what has been found in the handwriting it would appear reasonable to assume that he had come to terms with himself and lived a life of useful purpose, having found a measure of security in the face of change.

'Many thanks, you have done me proud and I have nothing to add' — Arthur Marshall

Sir John Gielgud, CH

Dear Mr. Holmes.

I have much pleasure in sending me a sample of my handwriting. I am right handed and have always written a very small type which seems to have shrunken alarmingly as I have got older!

Sincerely yours

John Gielgud

HANDWRITING HIGHLIGHTS

The isolated letters point to the use of intuition rather than logic, and the very small writing is indicative of considerable reserve. Arched or arcade form to the letters 'n' 'm' and 'h' show that form and deportment are important to him, as are strictly regulated social contacts. The letters 't' appear as a tick which means that he is fluent and adept at what he does, while an optimistic nature is clearly shown by the rising lines of writing. The cramped word spacing indicates that he is a private man who is economical, even parsimonious, in his approach to matters.

The letters are well simplified, and in this type of writing it means that the person penning the letters is a man of culture and refinement. This is further supported by the use of the Greek 'G' in the signature.

There are rather uneven pressure patterns, which point to an uncertain temper, but the efforts that have been made to make this small writing legible clearly show the inherent sincerity and kindness in his make-up.

PORTRAIT

Obviously cultured, undoubtedly conformist, Sir John Gielgud is also a man who likes to feel that he is in control of events and able to influence situations in which he might find himself. He is not disposed towards moodiness, although he can show ill temper on occasion, and as a general rule he tries to avoid emotional scenes, preferring instead to intellectualize any differences he has with others. In spite of this, he is capable of intense feeling which he keeps well controlled. There are no really strong ego ambitions or violent emotional reactions, which means that he has remarkably few prejudices, and tends to look at people and events with objectivity.

There is some introspection in his make-up, and at such times there is a reflective silence and a stifling of the feelings which has on occasion been responsible for his behaving outwardly in a rather elaborately contrived way, rather than allowing the spontaneous expression of his true self.

There is no genuine desire for social intercourse — in fact, there is a decided disinclination to mix with others. His mind is meditative and philosophical, and his personality is wrapped up in itself, so that whilst he has adapted to the demands of the outside world the adaptation is a forced one so that he might better maintain the form and deportment, both social and aesthetic, which he deems such an essential part of his life. He also exercises a firm control of his impulses, which control helps him greatly at those times when he needs to suppress his feelings in favour of his art.

He displays much initiative and effectiveness in his outward activities but, as stated earlier, he is somewhat inhibited in his emotional expression; emerging with this from the writing is a predisposition to concentrate upon the detail of a subject and study it profoundly. He prefers by far the outstanding isolated incident, to the same incident falling within a framework.

Highly intuitive, he can appraise and assess a situation quickly and reach a satisfactory conclusion without the need for much in the way of reasoning and logic. A friendly countenance is shown to the world, but rarely if ever are the thoughts behind the mask revealed, and he can at times appear remote and detached from what is happening around him, while all the time his sharp, discerning mind is absorbing the intricacies of what is occurring.

Being critical and self-reliant, he tends to show impatience when prevented from expressing himself, as he requires continuous freedom of thought and action to release his creativity. Rather excitable, undeniably reserved, difficult to get to know well, yet innately altruistic and kind, he has come to terms with the reality of his situation and lives his life to useful purpose, giving some preference to his private life over that of his career.

Sir John Gielgud is one of those rare persons who are passive and yet have achieved much. They never have to strive mightily to scale the peaks of their ambition, and they accomplish much with a minimum of effort. The secret is that they fit naturally into their chosen fields, they know what is required of them, and they know how to fulfil those requirements successfully.

Sir John has an added bonus in that he has enjoyed and still enjoys, every minute of his life. To be successful at what one enjoys is indeed achievement.

'Very accurate and perceptive . . . a good addition to my scrapbook' — Sir John Gielgud

Self-Control

Those who are able continuously to control the movements of their writing are also able to keep a tight rein on their emotions. Stroke direction is fairly constant, and the rhythm of the writing is vibrant. Height of the letters in the middle zone varies only slightly, and there are no fringed edges to the strokes.

Lady Mills (Mary Hayley Bell)

I was born Mary Hayley Bell but my name is also Mary Mills

HANDWRITING HIGHLIGHTS

The script is dominated by the upper and middle zones, and this domination strongly indicates intellectuality, good vision, and a social consciousness, and that everyday life plays a most important part in her overall existence. Well-controlled writing means well-controlled emotions, and well-simplified letters indicate that there is no fussiness in the make-up. The relaxed, flowing writing points to her lack of conformity and her fascination with new ideas and concepts. Left and right tendencies in the upper zone reveal her reflective and speculative mind, as well as her desire to build bridges between herself and others. Good horizontal tension of the strokes between letters certainly points to her competitive spirit and overall sense of purpose. A medium height of the letters in the middle zone clearly shows that her mind is well balanced.

The space between letters is quite wide, a sign of the lack of restriction in her social sphere. She needs room for herself, and likes to travel and to spend lavishly on food, clothing and hobbies. The script contains both arcade and wavy line forms of connection, showing the conflict between her creativity and her desire for form and convention. Medium pressure reveals her vitality and love of people, and reinforces the findings regarding her emotional stability and inner harmony. Christian and surnames are joined together, which clearly states that she is an individual and distinctive person.

PORTRAIT

As well as being a clear and lucid thinker, Lady Mills has the attributes of intellectual ease and adroitness so that her well-disciplined imagination is able to produce ideas that are both realistic and practical. Additionally, she is able to get to the heart of matters by eliminating the unnecessary and avoiding the detours of fantasy. There is, however, a natural impulsiveness which she feels she must control for fear that she might say or do something she will regret.

There is great interest in the world, and her urges are of the self-expressive kind so that there is little difficulty in establishing connections, whether practically in her relations with others or subjectively in her association of ideas. She has a great fondness for people and a complete lack of self-consciousness so that in her presence you would be continually entertained by conversation which is enlivened by her vitality and wide-ranging interests.

Generally an easygoing person, she demonstrates a clear dislike of routine for its own sake, and has a need for regular social stimulation.

Self-confident and well-adapted to reality, she possesses a balanced personality, and she can concentrate on an idea if she must, but she prefers action to meditation.

Her mind is mature, and constantly strives to maintain a balance in her affairs by rarely if ever allowing her to venture beyond her natural limitations thereby disposing her towards contentment and happiness. Her powers of endurance are good, and are enhanced by the careful use of available energy.

Artistically, there are a number of things she would still like to attempt but her needs in this direction have been sublimated to avoid friction with her existing commitments. Fortunately, her self-discipline is good and she has a liking for differentiation, so she can make distinctions in the moral, intellectual and aesthetic spheres of her life.

In her private and public lives she is the same person, and she has no inclination to assume a role in either: what you see is what she is — natural, sincere and unambiguous.

When it comes to travel and clothes, there is strongly indicated in her script some extravagance, which, while kept under control, is pleasurably indulged.

Lady Mills is indeed a most distinctive and individual person, and she expresses a genuine family pride that encompasses both her professional life as Mary Hayley Bell and her life as the devoted wife of Sir John Mills.

'Absolutely accurate . . . most delighted with it' — Lady Mills

Steve Race

It always seems to me that a person's
handwriting will to some degree depend
upon the dampness of his wrist coupled
with the roughness of the paper he uses.
In other words how smoothly his wrist
travels across the page. But then, I'm
no graphologist: merely —

Steve Race

HANDWRITING HIGHLIGHTS

This is a slow-to-medium-speed writing of good form
standard, which indicates the writer's good self-control.
The writing movements are not particularly well controlled, and this indicates a fluctuating emotional streak
that is not always kept in check. There is thoroughness
and precision in the way the letters are formed, which
points to him having the mind of a compiler. The stroke
angles oscillate, revealing a mixture of left, upright and
right slants, a clear sign that he is subject to contradictory
impulses; we can, therefore, detect frequent changes in
attitude to his social environment. There is pressure on

horizontal strokes, which depicts aggression, but overall the pressure pattern shows someone who is well-balanced and uncomplicated. The majority of words are finished with a short stroke of the pen, meaning that he can be abrupt, and the lean and narrow letters point to his rational mind and matter-of-fact approach to situations. The regularity of the writing proves that he can control the energies of his mind by force of will, and the unusualness of the writing indicates that he is a person who prefers to act independently. See how he uses the bar of the letter 't' to join the first name to the surname in his signature. This is a distinctive and individual gesture, reflecting these qualities in the man.

PORTRAIT

If the real Steve Race was asked to stand up, then the public and the private man would rise as one. What you see is what he is, talented, distinctive and individual with few if any pretensions, and with a well-balanced and uncomplicated mind that is both speculative and reflective. There is within that mind considerable mental activity, spurred on by ambition, which finds its outlet through the production of sound ideas. Logically, step by step, he is able to expose the essentials of a subject with the thoroughness of a compiler, and is well able to create a 'whole' from the information gleaned from a hundred authorities. His approach is orderly and, with the desire to think carefully, this gives him the ability to survey, to organize and to elucidate.

Impulsiveness is kept well under control, and matters generally are considered in a most profound manner. There has been a sound adjustment of the emotions to the intellect, and the now mature mind is ever open to new impressions and keen for fresh experiences and further knowledge.

200 *Stars in Their Own Write*

He is not an easy man to understand, and neither is he an easy man to please, but there is a vitality about him, and in his company one is never bored. As I mentioned earlier, there are few if any pretensions, and as a result he is not attracted to superficial people, preferring instead forthright relationships in both his professional and private lives.

Always prepared to take the initiative, he has developed a style of his own which allows him to express fully his individuality. There is no attempt to compromise with the world at the cost of his originality, and here he is supported by his disciplined will and a readiness to fight for his ideals. On occasions he can be headstrong, which can make him difficult to deal with.

The character is upright and somewhat inflexible, but this makes him reliable and thorough in everything he does. For better or worse, he is of one piece, being either for or against. Not for him the easy path of compromise, for he is a person with convictions, and since he has convictions he can, in turn, convince others. There is an unshakeable belief in himself and this endows him with an inner harmony. His steadfastness and firm sense of purpose mean that he is not easily swayed by new ideas and situations that have not had their merits and demerits thoroughly examined.

Although well able to make social contact, he does not depend upon others, and he does not court popularity, being quite content with his own company if necessary. Meeting him for the first time, you might sense a certain initial detachment, but as the relationship developed a warmth that is beneath the reserve would make itself felt.

There is concentration upon the realities of everyday life, and a striving to achieve and maintain a harmony of the mind by imposing restrictions upon himself. Always he is trying to give realization to things that are within his compass, and rarely if ever does he go beyond his capabilities. Thus he is well disposed towards contentment.

Although there tends to be a lack of consistent drive, there is an economical use of all his qualities in the fulfilment of his aims, and the endurance required to accomplish this is enhanced by the careful use of available energy. He is thereby able to establish a greater degree of purpose than is at first apparent. His curious and restless mind is capable of setting a goal some way ahead, and yet at the same time it is equally capable of industriously working towards an immediate target. Working for today whilst planning for tomorrow is a strong feature in the composition of this personality.

He is an aesthetic individual who displays strong artistic interests and abilities, and there is good taste, originality and a sense of proportion. The desire to be understood blends with a patient consideration of others, as he is a sincere person who does not think it necessary to conceal traits within himself or to distort or veil facts in any way. He has adjusted to the demands of his environment and has come to terms with himself in relation to reality. There is within him a liking for differentation, with a tendency to sacrifice his comfort to a conscious distinction which is applied to the moral, visual and intellectual spheres.

His pen strokes are those of the critic who shows concern for, and an understanding of, the abstract.

Steve Race has brought meaning, purpose, and a measure of stability to his life in the face of a changing world.

'I congratulate you and make a profound bow in the direction of your science' — Steve Race

Patrick Moore, CBE

Dear Mr. Holmes,

Just back from Australia – hence
the delay. At least I think that
my writing is legible, albeit slow –
I normally type everything. Quite
unusual for me to use a pen!

All good wishes,

Sincerely

Patrick Moore

HANDWRITING HIGHLIGHTS

That there are many angles present in the writing clearly depicts his relentless approach to a chosen course of action and the way in which he meets his difficulties head on. The constant size of the letters shows his stability, and honesty of purpose.

He is not an easygoing person, and will make quite fierce demands on himself and others, as may be seen from the very close spacing of most of the letters. The writing is quite rigid, and the strokes are in the main upright. From these features we can see that he is cautious in his dealings with others, and that he tries to exercise control and restraint over his environment as well as those with whom he is working.

PORTRAIT

An outstanding feature of this handwriting is the way in which it shows how the impulses of Patrick Moore are controlled by conscious will-power. It also clearly demonstrates that he is relentless both to himself and others in pursuit of a goal and that he makes no attempt whatsoever to shirk or avoid difficulties which he might find in his path. He is in fact unusually persevering, possessing a serious objective persistence. There is also the ability to focus, and to think up new and interesting ideas, which he can then take the initiative with and put into practice, and see through to a satisfactory conclusion.

He is a wilful person, and this can make him difficult to get along with, but his character is upright and even a bit starchy. The convictions are strong, and there is a firm belief in himself and in what he does. There is a preference for direct action and forceful argument, and on occasion these characteristics lean towards stubbornness and irascibility. Emotionally he is quite stable and lives well with himself; and he takes great care in his work, though, given the choice, he prefers to be involved in the active side of a project rather than being just a theoretical innovator. He is exceptionally well motivated in his work, and has the confidence to cope with most of the daily challenges of life, here greatly assisted by his exuberance and enthusiasm. His aims and ideals are rarely if ever in conflict, which reinforces his sense of realism. There is an easy intellectual ability and he much prefers his own way of thinking and presentation to that of others. The developed mind and pliable nature come from his intuitiveness, and whilst his mind is orderly he nevertheless has many moments of inspiration which he is able properly to associate and bring to fruition. Therefore, it would be right to assume that while he can pursue his work regularly and steadily, he can at the same time separate the important from the unimportant.

Sincere and with a fairly transparent character, he is an honest man, totally without falsehood and ambiguity. He wants to be fully understood by others, and to that end he has developed a clear and lucid form of expression, and is frank in his views and objectives about his work. There is a liking, or even a preference, for thinking in the abstract and his powers of reasoning and abstraction means that he is interested more in ideas than in people. As a result he might appear self-contained, even diffident, but in reality he is quite friendly, although he does not allow people to get too close as he is not particularly emotional or responsive.

He is prudent in the manner in which he conducts his affairs, and as his self-control is consciously applied, he is able to choose whether or not to unbend and let himself go. The show of friendliness which he puts on when the need arises, is, however, rarely if ever the spontaneous expression of his inner feelings. From time to time he experiences some difficulty with people, and he can find himself disappointed by their actions or reactions, and the fact that they do not always live up to his expectations.

Somewhat unconventional, he dislikes any form of restriction or restraint, having a need for freedom of thought in his everyday activities. This is partly due to the fact that he is a real livewire both mentally and physically, with many schemes being thought up and brought to a conclusion. In fact, he needs exaggerated activity to satisfy his longings, and without it he would become querulous and indulge in violent opposition for its own sake.

Patrick Moore is a very distinctive and individual person, and it is hardly surprising that he has chosen the universe as his subject — for what else could possibly satisfy the industriousness of this man?

Bill Owen

Dear Mr. Holmes,

Herewith a sample of my scribble

I hope it will suffice. I write

with my right hand.

Yours sincerely,

Bill Owen

HANDWRITING HIGHLIGHTS

The fact that his thoughts dwell on past events and people he has known is clearly revealed in this script by the leftward tendencies in the middle zone of the writing. His penetrating insight into human activities and his energetic and reliable approach to work are demonstrated by the legibility and the rightward slant, plus the good connection of letters and the even pressure. Assertiveness and obstinacy are represented by the long lower strokes, and self-centredness is indicated by the short final strokes at the end of the majority of words. Good taste and a sense of proportion are revealed by capital letters that display the same qualities. Except in the signature there are no inflated loops anywhere in the writing, and this points to his thoughts being rational and his approach to events cool, matter-of-fact and realistic.

The irregular height of the upper zone strokes shows that he has a mind that is restless and filled with curiosity, and the weak bars to the letters 't' proclaim that he is influenced rather easily. He can be inconsiderate of the feelings of others, as may be seen by the neglect of certain letters.

PORTRAIT

Perhaps the most important feature emerging from the handwriting of Bill Owen is that of his penetrating insight into human relationships and activities. Certainly he is a man who is interested in what is happening around him, and he is socially active and aware with a real liking for, and an interest in, people. Because he is able to reveal his feelings to others he can elicit a response from them, and this in turn has contributed to his understanding.

He has a mature, realistic outlook on life, and he evaluates most events in a balanced manner. His thinking is rational and consistent, and his approach to his work is purposeful. His ideas are, therefore, sound and he is able to develop them in his mind logically, step by step.

Strong feelings are consciously restrained for the sake of formality, and because his fear of emotional involvement, and this unwillingness to unbend and let go leads to some strain. His self-confidence is strong, but it can fluctuate occasionally although the causal insecurities are kept well hidden. It would appear, therefore, that under the air of self-confidence and calm there is some tension, which could, of course, account for occasional bouts of moodiness and irritability. At such times he would appear patronizing, self-centred and somewhat inconsiderate; this is just a form of self-protection, though, and soon passes. He can be assertive and obstinate when he defends his conventional habits and beliefs, but there is always aim and determination in what he does. He is well adapted to his work and has justified pride in what he has so far achieved.

He reflects much on the past and finds it difficult either to give up or to forget those people who have meant much to him in the past.

Bill Owen has come to terms with himself in relation to the reality of his life, and now lives it to useful purpose within the limitations he has himself imposed. Thus he has found a measure of security in the face of change.

Sir Alastair Burnet

Dear Mr Holmes,

Thank you for your letter of January 27th. Although I must say that I'm mildly sceptical about what can be learned from handwriting — apart, I suppose, from the relative inebriation of the writer — I'm glad to pen these lines to you myself, and will await, with suitable apprehension, your conclusions.

Yours sincerely,

Alastair Burnet.

I am right-handed.

HANDWRITING HIGHLIGHTS

Whatever might be said to the contrary, this handwriting clearly shows that Sir Alastair Burnet is not a man who courts popularity, and this can be seen by the way in which he changes letter forms to a style all his own. The tension in the writing clearly indicates that he is a cautious and conformist person and also a worrier who likes to feel that he is in control of events. The middle zone is small, and this, in addition to the tapering characteristics of many words, speaks volumes for his discretion and diplomatic skill. Although the stroke slant varies quite considerably, the writing is generally well controlled and this tells us that he has an excitable temperament which he keeps tightly suppressed.

The space between letters varies considerably, and from this we can deduce that he has a somewhat variable approach to life and is quite capable of swinging from tolerance to intolerance, and from self-assuredness to nervous uncertainty. A tendency to lose his temper is revealed by the heavy pressure patterns that appear throughout the handwriting

There is about the script a superficial impression of rhythm, and this confirms that there is an inherent excitability of temperament, which is generally controlled and creatively directed.

PORTRAIT

One of the outstanding features of Sir Alastair Burnet is his ability to organize and critically arrange matters, connecting them in such a way as to be able to give form and meaning to their abstract qualities. The resulting orderliness has played no small part in his success, and has been made possible by his ability to control his natural impulses through the strength of his will. The outcome of this creative discipline is that, even in embryo, his ideas are both realistic and practical so that, when they are further processed through his analytical mind with its capacity for reasoning and logic, it is hardly surprising that the resulting judgements are to be relied upon.

There is within him an underlying excitability of temperament, which is generally well controlled and creatively directed; beneath the air of calm and self-confidence, however, there is some strife. He is not a man to reveal his innermost thoughts and feelings and he keeps a tight rein on his emotions, but when he does 'go up in the air' there is quite likely to be a fiery display of anger.

He is a worrier who likes to impose as much control as

possible on his working environment, and he attempts to intellectualize problems which would respond better to more subjective handling — he has a belief that more control can be brought to bear if the difficulty is turned into an academic exercise. His equanimity is made manifest through a combination of will-power and intellect, both of which play an important part in the way he conducts his life. One could describe him as a cautious conformist, conventional in both dress and manner and with a liking for tradition and a tendency towards the orthodox.

He has adapted well to the outside world without ever disclosing much about his inner self. He is not particularly interested in popularity for its own sake, and will say or do nothing which goes against his natural inclinations. Critical and self-reliant, he is obstinately determined to stand by his rights and principles, and, with this strength, in addition to his realistic approach, he is a man who makes no attempt to shirk responsibility.

There is a fluctuating desire to socialize, and relationships are developed with some caution. His naturally sympathetic outlook towards the troubles of others has made him develop discretionary and diplomatic skills as a defence against the sentimentality which is so much a part of his character. A rather unassuming man, he does not give too great a prominence to either his public or his private life, and his modesty is that of an able mind.

Sir Alastair Burnet has come to terms with himself, and has found satisfaction and a measure of security in the face of the troublesome and changing world of which he is so much a part.

'Although you are accurate in seeing the essential dullness of my life, there are one or two points of excitability which make it all worthwhile' — Sir Alastair Burnet

Frank Muir, CBE

Dear Mr. Holmes,

*Here, with pleasure, are a
few lines of my handwriting. Written in
some haste with a Pentel Stylo.
All good wishes,*

Frank Muir

HANDWRITING HIGHLIGHTS

The somewhat stiff and rigid writing means that Frank Muir likes to have as much control as possible over his environment, and the narrow spacing between letters points to the fact that he does not find it easy to let go. The good legibility of virtually all words and letters, in or out of context, displays his consideration for others, and his honesty of purpose and intent. His love of order and method is illustrated by the excellent spacing between both words and lines, and the strong even pressure shows that he has an even-tempered approach to life. Instinctive feelings and idealistic dreams are indicated by the long swing of the lower loops to the letters 'g' and 'y'.

To see the harmonious writing is to see that same quality in the character of Frank Muir, and his liking of the impressive and ornamental is also easily recognizable, as is the fact that he will always arrange things aesthetically and never vulgarly.

PORTRAIT

Once you got to know Frank Muir you would be aware of his peaceable temperament and his love of order and method. His aims and ideals are not in conflict, which makes his personality harmonious and his outlook and behaviour both positive and genuine. He desires to be understood, and as he has the ability for clear expression this makes him a good speaker and stylist, efficient in the sphere of practical life. He is a considerate man, honest and open, with a penetrating insight into the human condition. He pursues his work steadily and concentrates upon it, working purposefully and according to a plan. There is a strong self-control which makes him level-headed and thoughtful, and because of the ability to concentrate and focus his mind he is able to think in an even, consistent and logical manner and to act in a systematic way.

The mature mind is ever open to new impressions and eager for fresh experiences and further knowledge. He can conceive ideas and then assume the initiative so that his reliable and thorough nature is in a position to take to completion that which he starts.

A man of cultured taste and intellectuality, rather conservative in outlook, and yet . . . there is in him a liking for the impressive and the ornamental. As his sense for the essential has been developed tastefully, however, he will always arrange things aesthetically, never vulgarly.

Being a rational thinker with a fine critical sense, he tends to be rather cool and matter-of-fact even though he possesses an artistically creative imagination. Instinctive feelings and idealistic dreams probably influence him much more than do the demands of social contact, but there is a need for people and he is keen to adapt himself. To this end he has developed an active social awareness and he enjoys meeting people, showing a love of and zest for life. His interests focus mainly on people and their behaviour, and it is through the stimulation of his ideas and the reassurance he gets from others that he can realize and measure his worth. Although he has adapted well to the demands of others he does not easily disclose his inner feelings, and he believes strongly in the need for form and deportment. Personal questions are therefore answered with great reserve, and he will sometimes overcompensate in his reaction to them by becoming nonchalant. He does like his social relations to be quite strictly regulated — not for him the surprise event where he might, albeit momentarily, lose control.

He can be quite relentless with himself and others as he advances towards a given goal, and at these times the world will have to adapt itself to his needs. There is an urge towards continuous activity which comes from unstilled ambition and a dissatisfaction with that so far achieved. The ambition, though, is not exaggerated or exorbitant as, because he is quite honest in his endeavours to achieve something good and worthwhile, if he is disappointed in his efforts, he is able to accept the outcome without rancour or bitterness.

His is a disciplined imagination that is not easily swayed by new ideas or situations, so that he is aware of his aim and purpose and this makes him goal-minded. With his strongly disciplined will, he is willing and able to fight for his ideals, and on these occasions he can be terse and sharp-tongued.

Briefly, Frank Muir is a rather cautious and conformist worrier who likes to feel that he is in control of whatever he is undertaking. His moods are fairly even and consistent, but when he does let go it is likely to result in quite a show of frustration and anger. He has good powers of concentration, and is excellent at work requiring attention to detail while he does not particularly like tasks where there is a risk of things getting out of hand. He finds it difficult to express his deepest emotions and he tends to bottle up hurt feelings and wounded pride. Because of this he will usually try to intellectualize an argument as this way he feels that he has more control over what is happening. Conscientiousness is the real keystone of his character and one feels that his motto should be: 'If a job's worth doing, it's worth doing well' — and it wouldn't surprise me if he were to add 'whether you are paid for it or not'.

'I read your analysis with increasing astonishment and thought it very accurate but my wife tells me it is uncannily precise' — Frank Muir

Sociability

Rounded middle zone letters, a moderate right slant, a proportionately large middle zone, wide letters and stroke fluency all point to the writer's desire for an interesting social life.

Ernie Wise, OBE

Dear Derek.

Thankyou for your letter.
I am enclosing a sample of my
Lad writing written with a ait of a
dof a biro. I an aight Landed
ad its my opinion he should learn
to write with both Laan.

Yours Sincerly
Ernie Wisean.

HANDWRITING HIGHLIGHTS

Unusual letter forms point to a desire to follow his own wishes, and the very uneven pressure pattern demonstrates that he is well able to lose his temper. The slant of the letters to the right is quite pronounced and indicates a dependency on others. Starting strokes in the script point to conformity and the many small letters which appear in the midst of those of normal size are a sign of uncertainties and fears kept well hidden. There are few if any strokes that either descend well below the writing line or ascend much above it, and this clearly signals that the main interests of Ernie Wise are in his work and everyday life.

The tapering characteristic of many words and letters points to shrewdness and a business-minded approach in his dealings with others, and this is reinforced by the capital 'I's', which have the appearance of the figure nine, a sure sign of his concern for matters financial.

PORTRAIT

The handwriting of Ernie Wise reveals that he is a realist, and this realism combined with his mature approach to life, indicates that he is always trying to give realization to things within his scope. This of course means that generally he is well disposed towards contentment. There is also a preoccupation with the present, the here-and-now, and a tendency to take life much as it comes. Daydreaming and flights of fancy are rare features in this moderate, level-headed man's make-up, as his thoughts are in the main purposeful and systematic, making his ideas sound and his perception relevant.

He is certainly of an independent disposition, and exercises good control over his feelings and impulses, as indeed he does over all his activities. He enjoys his own company, has a liking for material success, and is far more interested in his daily work than in anything else. He has a creative mind and would rather adapt himself to various differing situations than force himself to follow one rigid path.

He needs to be able to express himself freely, and inclines towards extroversion, which accounts for his liking of attractive clothes and his wish for an interesting social life. His active social awareness, combined with some compliance with conventional standards of behaviour and a genuine enjoyment of meeting people, means that he only rarely experiences difficulty in making contact with others.

He is an ambitious man with a love of life and an inner strength which enable him to pursue with enthusiasm that which he enjoys. The stimulation of his ideas, with the reassurance he gets from others, enable him to measure his worth. He is an emphatic and gesticulating speaker who loves to be centre stage and he really comes alive when there is an audience to stimulate his ideas.

There is concentration upon the self, which can sometimes lead to a lack of consideration for others, usually when he is pursuing some aim. He needs to be his own man, and is not easily influenced by others, and this makes him stubborn, outspoken and even argumentative. There is also an impatient side to his nature so that when he is needlessly delayed or frustrated, he can fly off the handle and become for a while downright unneighbourly.

There are feelings of doubt and uncertainty but they are kept well hidden and, his disposition being somewhat changeable, he can be moody and view life with some inconsistency — seeing situations in detail one day, and generalizing about them the next. He is, however, a positive person, though, like many talented and thoughtful people, there is an underlying uncertainty which springs from the feeling that he has not always made the most of past opportunities.

He is rather sensitive to external impressions, and his sensitivity towards criticism in particular has taught him to be shrewd and diplomatic in his dealings with others.

Ernie Wise has come to terms with himself, giving his life some meaning and purpose, but that does not mean that there are no hills left to climb or rivers to cross, for we can see quite clearly in this talented man's handwriting that there are.

'I think it's fine' — Ernie Wise

Gloria Hunniford

Dear Derek,
It was a great
pleasure to hear
from you and
I would like
to wish you
well with your
book.
Love
Gloria
x

G H

HANDWRITING HIGHLIGHTS

The writing is both small and wide, and this combination indicates a need for plenty of room to accommodate an expansive nature, and shows that caution and reserve are also present. The rounded letters of the middle zone point to her warm-heartedness, and the upright nature of the strokes tells of her self-control. She is not particularly easygoing, as is shown by the close positioning of the letters, and the straight lines of writing are a clear sign of her steadfastness. The rising strokes of letters such as 'f' and 't' do not extend very far above the baseline of the writing and neither do the lower strokes of letters such as 'g' and 'y' venture far below. This concentration on the central or middle zone of the script points to a liking for work as well as everyday life. The relaxed style employed in forming the letters tell us that she is a real laid-back lady who likes to kick over the traces occasionally. She is also attracted by new ideas and concepts and prefers working with people who are not too conformist in their attitudes.

PORTRAIT

Gloria Hunniford is very much her own woman, and if her role demands that she wear conventional dress she will all the time be yearning to wear casual, individualistic clothes, and longing to kick over the traces. She loves things that are original and unusual and it is near impossible for her to get stuck in a rut for too long; indeed, she will avoid people or tasks that restrict her creative impulses. As she does not keep her emotions on too tight a rein, she can be excitable and vivacious, moody, or impulsive, blurting out things which later she wishes she had kept to herself.

Her social life dominates all other activities, and as this is at the expense of the instinctive and intellectual sides of her nature, there is a need to increase the range of her mind by widening her interests. Although the outlook is independent there is nevertheless a dependency on the world around her, as in spite of the control she is not too well anchored in herself. She is a warm-hearted person who tends to control her relationships with others rather tightly as she suffers some emotional turmoil. Matter-of-fact and objective, she thinks in a consistent way, is helpful, and is socially compatible, being uncomplicated and neither retiring nor pushy.

She is quite good at determining future eventualities as she has the ability to assess the possibilities in a given situation in advance. There is enough energy to carry through her plans quickly and with zest once she has made her decision, and here she is helped by her devotion to saving time and reducing unnecessary effort. Used to thinking in the abstract, she can easily connect and arrange matters in her mind, and in many instances she can make sense out of apparent nonsense.

Enthusiastic and full of nervous energy, she is tense and talkative so that she appears animated, lively and not a little impatient. At the same time, she is sensitive, mature, and concerned with the realities of life, and does not indulge in exaggerated self-observation. She has come to terms with her life and has developed a measure of security in an insecure environment. Her natural instinct is to be liberal and sympathetic, but because of circumstances she has to simulate the disciplined and concentrated worker. Although to some extent she has rid herself from the effects of the past, she has not been able to digest its influences completely. There is, as a result, some inhibition of the instincts, giving rise to caution and secretiveness and making her cover up her tracks and hide something of herself from the world. There is indeed a determination not to reveal herself clearly and definitely. There is, however, nothing pretentious about Gloria Hunniford and what you see is what she is both in private and in public. Maybe this fact comes across in her dealings with people, and contributes in no small way to her success.

'The profile was incredibly accurate . . . overall a very very perceptive analysis' — Gloria Hunniford

Richard Briers

Dear Derek Holmes _
Thanks so much for your request.
I am right handed and wish
you best of luck with my
personality portrait

    Best Wishes

    Richard Briers
    _

HANDWRITING HIGHLIGHTS

There is little conflict between the public and private lives, as evidenced by the identical penning of the forename and surname. The writing is fairly legible, although some letters when taken out of context are difficult even to decipher. From this we can assume that he is a sincere and considerate man who nevertheless has a need to develop a style of his own. The writing concentrates on the middle zone, the lower loops of letters such as 'y' rarely venturing far down, and the upper strokes to letters such as 't' rarely flying high. This concentration on the middle of the writing shows that he is chiefly preoccupied with everyday matters, and strives to maintain a balance in his affairs by rarely if ever going beyond his natural limitations. The letter slant is somewhat variable, and this factor indicates the presence of conflict within the psyche, while the uneven pressure pattern confirms this in so far as it tells of the occasional loss of temper. This is fluent handwriting and could only be that of a man who is able to express his ideas fluently.

PORTRAIT

Richard Briers' main desires are to express his individuality and to develop a style that is uniquely his own. He is fortunate that he can achieve both aims through his abilities for clear and lucid expression and clarity of thought. He has adjusted to the demands of his world, and brought order into his affairs, and, as a sincere and considerate man, wishes to understand and in turn to be understood.

He is fascinated by new ideas and by the unusual and unfamiliar and, being best suited to tasks and projects requiring imagination and creativity, he finds routine rather irksome. He does tend to be impulsive on occasion, saying and doing things on the spur of the moment and afterwards having reason for regret. But, although he is fundamentally an emotional person, he is generally able to control his feelings; this subduing of his natural impulses, however, can make him difficult both to understand and to please. There is no pretension in his make-up and he dislikes superficiality in both his private and his professional life.

He is very much a realist whose whole approach reflects the modesty of his able mind, and whilst his general outlook on life is positive, his self-assurance occasionally falters, allowing in the doubts and bringing on a somewhat moody and reflective atmosphere. He has to work at his air of self-confidence as he is not always as relaxed as he at first appears.

He will make a real effort not to hurt people's feelings and is able to exercise tact at just the right time, knowing instinctively when he has made his point and taking it just so far and no farther.

His mature mind is chiefly occupied with everyday matters and, while there is a constant striving to achieve, he maintains a balance in his life by imposing limits upon himself and rarely ever attempting to go beyond his natural capabilities. Thus he is able to bring a degree of contentment and happiness into his life. Although independent and self-reliant, he does require recognition in order to give of his best, but being in the main critical of group standards, he is consequently a bit of a loner. There are deep feelings towards others but he has difficulty in showing them until a relationship has developed sufficiently, although he is well able to put on an initial show of friendliness at a fairly superficial level.

He is a tense yet enthusiastic man who finds relaxation difficult, driven by his active imagination to set and attain objectives, his nervous ardour colouring all his activities. Imagination and external impressions both have a great effect upon him, and, indeed, are at the seat of his creative powers. To safeguard the mobility of his many-sided personality he makes an effort to avoid moulding his character along more conventional lines.

His sharp, discerning mind needs freedom of thought the better to express his abundance of ideas fluently and without restraint, and he is not too considerate of anything which does not further this end. If restraint is placed upon his attempts at expression then he will withdraw and give the appearance of not being 'with it'.

He has a justified pride in his achievements, and displays an optimistic view of the future, but this is tempered with the realization that he has not always made the most of past opportunities.

The professional and public life is pretty well in balance with the private life, and it is reasonable to assume that Richard Briers has come to terms with himself in relation to the reality of his achievements and has, therefore, found a measure of security.

'I am delighted with it and my wife says it's surprisingly accurate' — Richard Briers

Barbara Windsor

Dear Derek,
      Just to say I am
right-handed and just become
the owner of the "Plough Inn"
      All the best
            Love
                  Barbara Windsor x

HANDWRITING HIGHLIGHTS

The middle zone dominates this handwriting and clearly points to how much she values her everyday social life. The words and letters are both clearly legible, demonstrating the transparency of her character and the need to be understood. The script has a free flowing quality, and into this can be read her liking for the unusual and unfamiliar and the fact that she dislikes routine for its own sake. The strong slope to the right indicates her active social awareness as well as her love of people, and these traits are further indicated by the medium pressure of the script. Pressure is constant throughout the long strokes which penetrate all three zones, and from this we can deduce her strength of will, headstrongness and ability to take the initiative in her dealings with others. The large capital 'I' reveals self-assurance, but being placed close to the following word it shows that she should not have to undergo long periods of solitude. The clearly read signature states that what you see is what she is. A natural woman, free of all pretensions.

PORTRAIT

There is considerably more depth to the personality of Barbara Windsor than one might at first sight imagine, and if you got to know her well you would soon discover the rather earnest, self-critical side to her nature that tends to make her somewhat over-conscientious about whatever it is that is currently engaging her interest.

Her spontaneous and natural mind makes her less conformist than most, and she loves to kick over the traces occasionally. The unfamiliar fascinates her, and she is in her element when carrying out tasks requiring creative imagination — one could say that novelty and change are for her the spices of life.

Although usually tolerant and warm-hearted, she can become irritable and moody through occasional feelings of uncertainty, and at these times she can blurt out remarks with little thought for the consequences. Overall, she has a strong and positive personality, and an uncompromising obstinacy when defending her convictions and principles, which enables her to carry through her ideas even against quite vigorous opposition.

A mature outlook makes her thorough and reliable in what she does, particularly if her interest in and enthusiasm for a project can be maintained. Above all, she believes in herself, and this belief is the source of her inner strength, making her steadfast and persistent so that she doesn't attempt to shirk or avoid responsibilities. She overcomes obstacles and resistance rather than adapting smoothly to them.

She has a desire to be understood by others, and in turn her words are unambiguous and clear, as her character is transparent. This honesty of purpose helps her to express her individuality and to develop further her own distinctive style. She is extremely active, with varied interests, and carries within herself strong feelings of accomplishment. These traits, when combined with the occasional over-enthusiastic approach, can blind her to possible problems which are looming.

Her everyday life is important to her as she has a highly developed social awareness and enjoys meeting people and demonstrating clearly how she feels towards them. She has a great love of and a zest for life, and always present is the strong need for freedom of thought and action, which, if it is restricted for too long, will make her restless and not a little unneighbourly.

Talkative and gregarious, her natural tendency is to dominate a relationship although she does make an attempt to be neither too pushy nor too offhand, and, as she is relatively well balanced and uncomplicated, she mostly succeeds. She thrives when with others, and she requires their stimulation to make her function effectively.

She has learned to come to terms with the reality of her situation and has found a measure of security in the face of change.

Close friends of hers would tell you that Barbara Windsor is without pretension and that what you see is what she is, both in public and in private. She is true to herself, and whilst she is a woman of considerable charm and attraction I am sure that you will now agree that she is not *just* a pretty face.

'Very like me. An excellent likeness' — Barbara Windsor

Una Stubbs

Dear Derek

Thank you for your letter.
I too am very interested in handwriting
as one of my sons studies calligraphy.
Every success with your book
it should be very interesting.

Sincerely
Una Stubbs

P.S. I am left handed.

HANDWRITING HIGHLIGHTS

This writing is nearly all middle zone, with virtually no
lower loops to letters such as 'g' or 'y' and no rising strokes
as part of the letters 't' 'h' or 'k'. The concentration in the
central area means that the primary interests are in her
work and her everyday life. Meditation and reflection
on the past are indicated by the leftward swing of the
top stroke of the letters 'd' and the way in which the
underlengths of the letters 'y' and 'g' are open to the left.
The rigid writing means conventionality, and the angles
which go towards forming letters such as 'n', 'm' and

'h' clearly show that she tackles her problems head-on and does not shirk responsibility. In spite of her being left-handed, which tends to cause letters to slope to the left, these letters slant to the right, and this really shows her need for contact with other people. The letters are very close together, which more than any other factor means that she is not an easygoing person.

The pressure is strong, pointing to good energy potential, but some tremulous strokes indicate a nerviness present in the make-up. Feelings of guilt or remorse are revealed by the way in which the capital letters 'I' are bent over in what looks like a foetal position.

PORTRAIT

Cautious and not too willing to take risks, Una Stubbs is a worrier about situations where she feels she might not be able to exercise total control. As a result, she rarely applies subjective judgements in these cases, preferring instead to intellectualize the difficulties.

She has a straightforward approach to life, which leads her to express opinions openly, unhesitatingly and even dogmatically, to the point where she can have difficulty in accepting the logical conclusions of others if they conflict with her own views. As she is self-sufficient, her thoughts and ideas are of greater importance to her than is generally considered the norm, and as she will not compromise her individuality she can be quite uncooperative at times.

She meets difficulties head-on, making no attempt to avoid her responsibilities, and she is as relentless towards herself as she is towards others when pursuing a goal. She is an unusually persistent and perservering worker, and her exacting approach does not permit weak compromise towards herself, so that once she has started a project she will see it through to a satisfactory conclusion.

She is capable of intense feelings, and there is a need to express them, but as she is not one to wear her heart on her sleeve she will counter them either by denying their existence or by tightly controlling them. Another way she has of dissipating them is through her art.

It is difficult for her to be truly objective as she has a highly developed imagination, and self-control has to be strongly applied to discipline her impressionability. There is an urge for contact with others and a need for sociability, and she can, if she is not too careful, be unduly influenced by those with whom she comes into contact.

She does not always show the confident fluency of which she is capable, and there is some need to escape from the uncertainties and doubts which beset her by indulging in both physical and mental introspection. There is some looking inwards and to the past, and an examination of what might have been, so that in spite of the fact that she has made many adjustments she is still frequently disturbed by longings that are not always clearly defined.

There is a pessimistic side to her nature, and a tendency to look on the dark side, which can act as a deterrent to going ahead with new ideas. Her main preoccupation is with the present and she takes things as they come, only rarely giving way to flights of fancy. There is both modesty and moderation, and she tries hard to reach and maintain a harmony of the mind by always trying to achieve those things which lie within her range. As she rarely if ever attempts to go beyond her scope she remains unassuming and, in a way, content.

There is manual skill, which is used in a constructive way, and when this is combined with the facts that she has an eye for detail and an ability to concentrate it leads one to suppose that her hobbies would include some pastime requiring total absorption, such as lace-making or fine needlework.

Una Stubbs is ambitious, and will use her assertive nature to achieve her wishes, but because of her conventional outlook those wishes have to be achieved according to prescribed methods — she will not, for instance, try to get ahead by challenging legitimate authority or accepted custom.

Like most people, she enjoys success and she will try her hardest to improve her position, but success at any price is not what she wants and there is a price she is not prepared to pay. One can only respect her the more for that.

'Oh crumbs! Am I really like that?' — Una Stubbs

Roy Castle

Dear Derek,

I don't know what you can make of this scribble — in fact, I doubt if I can make it last four lines without having to lie down.

If it's bad — blame Des O'Conner.

Cheers

Roy Castle

HANDWRITING HIGHLIGHTS

Examine the signature carefully, and you will see that the forename is quite illegible whilst the surname is easily read. This indicates that Roy Castle keeps his personal life private and away from the gaze of his public. The writing is large — a sign of ebullience and self-confidence, like the strong bars crossing the letter 't' about half-way up the stem. This is a very fluent script, which points to the same quality being present in his personality, and the consistent way in which the writing is executed means that the person who penned it must also be consistent and purposeful in his approach to work. The middle zone dominates, and this clearly demonstrates a preference for everyday life, while the strong slant of the letter stokes to the right proclaims his need and affection for others. The layout is good, so he has accepted his limitations and lives his life to useful purpose. The middle zone letters are full, so we can safely assume that he is a kind, warm-hearted person whose soul and feeling are expressed as a full ego.

PORTRAIT

Roy Castle really enjoys meeting people, and his main interest in life centres on his contact with others and the way in which they respond to him. It is through those responses that he gains his fulfilment and satisfaction. His handwriting also reflects maturity and a readiness to take an interest in a diverse range of activities. He is a moderate man who does not yearn for that which is beyond him and as a result he is happy and content. He loves his freedom and is keen to take advantage of all that is offered, particularly when it helps him to satisfy his need to express his creativity and individuality.

He is an energetic man who works hard and has the ability to concentrate upon the job in hand, and additionally he knows instinctively what is and what is not important. Most effective when working on his own, he prefers to have personal, rather than shared, authority, as if he has to seek too much approval from others for his actions he becomes rather unsettled and anxious. He can be quite firm when dealing with people, but usually manages to disguise it with tactfulness; nevertheless, when pursuing a current project he can be quite uncompromising. His life and work are much influenced by will-power and intellect, and since he is emotionally stable these factors make him invariable in his approach. He is in many ways an independent man who enjoys his own company and is not swayed easily by the points of view of others.

Whilst the personality is outgoing, there is a part of him that he holds back; a part that reflects on the past; a form of emotional reticence that can, when its influences are strong, prevent him expressing himself in a totally genuine manner. In general, though, the sensitiveness that is so much a part of him has been mastered and brought under control.

He is an earnest and self-critical person who acts in a positive manner, displaying confidence in his decisions. There is a sincere, quick and intelligent mind that is able to cope with abstract ideas, which are expressed freely, and as he is logical and concerned with essentials, it means that he has a good head for business matters. Being a highly discriminating individual with a liking for the impressive and ornamental, he can be susceptible to flattery. He has a strong desire to help others but, fortunately, there is a controlling firmness in his make-up that keeps him from being exploited.

Roy Castle is a good speaker and stylist with an ability for clear and lucid expression, and a sincere wish to be thoroughly understood by others. As he has no desire whatsoever to hide from the world, it means that he has all the qualities of the first-rate entertainer.

Understanding

The natural psychologists, those who instinctively understand the human condition, frequently make capital letters, particularly those that appear in their signature, span all three zones of the writing. This expansiveness reveals a liking for dwelling fully in all spheres of existence and contributes much to their understanding of the emotional, intellectual, spiritual and instinctive lives of themselves and others.

Ronnie Corbett, OBE

Dear Jack,

Many thanks for your kind letter and, indeed your interest in my hideous scrawl — I am by the way right handed.

Ronnie Corbett

HANDWRITING HIGHLIGHTS

The writing clearly demonstrates an undeviating impulse to the right, clearly pointing to the unstilled ambition and the feeling that there is yet more to be achieved. There is a spontaneity about the writing that indicates strongly the same quality about the actions of the man. Capital letters that descend into the lower zone point to his being a born practical psychologist with a ready understanding of the human condition.

The rising line of the signature shows that he has the confidence to cope with the problems of everyday life, and the strong bars to the letters 't' say quite clearly that he is strong-minded and likes his own way.

PORTRAIT

Within the psyche of Ronnie Corbett there is the craving of unstilled ambition; the feeling that there is more to be achieved, and this makes him restlessly press on to try to discover new and better things. He is mentally and physically active, and he gives freely of himself when in pursuit of that which affords him satisfaction. The drive is consistent, and yet there are pauses for reflection which enable him to take stock. There is strong self-discipline and good control of the feelings and impulses, which enables him to be purposeful in his approach to life; in spite of this, however, he remains at heart a sensitive and rather reserved man. He is fairly easygoing and not too much of a conformist, and this is reflected in his love of new ideas and of concepts which embrace the unusual and unfamiliar. Necessary routine he can live with, but needless restraint, especially if it is applied rigidly, is met with moodiness and irritability. He requires regular stimulation in order to function properly, and this can also lead to his acting on the spur of the moment. His mind is developed and his nature pliable and not particularly selfish, but for all that he is not an especially considerate man and to achieve his aims he will pressurize others to what might seem to them an unreasonable extent. He will not compromise his individuality, as popularity for its own sake does not interest him. When defending his views and opinions he can become quite heated and obstinate to the point where he forgets discipline. Generally, he displays good taste and a sense of proportion in his dealings with others.

He likes to think things over, and he is able to concentrate on the matter in hand even under difficult circumstances. Assertiveness is very much a feature of his make-up, and he appears confident in his relationships with others. He will launch into a conversation with a stranger and even if his initial overtures are rebuffed he will not be deterred.

Ronnie Corbett is a natural, optimistic and friendly person with a balancing control of firmness in his personality; he is fond of people and should not be compelled to undergo long periods of solitude. Privately or publicly, he behaves the same, and it is clear from his writing that the two lives are well-balanced, with neither detracting from the other.

There is some reflecting on the past, a time that has some specific meaning for him, and arising from this is a secretiveness which compels him to hide his private thoughts from even his nearest associates. He has a deep understanding of, and feeling for, people. An independent person, confident in his ability to cope with everything that life can throw at him, he is undoubtedly intelligent, with an orderly mind well able to think carefully and in the abstract.

One of the most outstanding features of Ronnie Corbett is his determination to stand on his own two feet and ask for nothing from others. Perhaps if he leaned more on others the conflict between his desire to break new ground and his wish to stay secure in the less alien environment of the known would be less fierce.

Barbara Cartland

You are what you eat

You become what you think

Barbara Cartland

Right hand!

HANDWRITING HIGHLIGHTS

Capital letters, particularly those of the signature, drop deep into the lower zones of the writing, and this is highly indicative of someone who understands the spiritual qualities residing, one hopes, within us all. The writing has one of the highest graphological form standards that I have examined to date, and this a sure pointer to her high intelligence. The marvellous simplification of the letters shows that she cuts through the waffle and gets down to basics, and the horizontal lines of writing reveal equanimity. The good spacing between the words and between the lines point to an orderly mind, and the even size of middle zone letters speaks clearly of assuredness and self-confidence. The relaxed writing shows her love of the unfamiliar and indeed anything that offers a challenge. The writing of the signature is identical to the rest of the script and has, therefore, been written by someone who is natural and unpretentious.

PORTRAIT

Barbara Cartland has a deep understanding of the spiritual qualities surrounding the human condition, though this in itself would not account for her achievements.

In her mind she is constantly conceiving ideas, which are then brought into the light of day by her initiative, to have applied to them the energy and persistence necessary to see them through to a successful conclusion. No inhibitions stand in the way of her natural and instinctive desire for expression and communication, so there is purposefulness and certainty of aim, which is further assisted by the fact that she does not indulge in exaggerated self-observation.

The restless mind is filled with curiosity about much that is happening in the world, and the outlook is, therefore, speculative rather than reflective. Diplomacy, versatility, originality and constructiveness are all present in the well-ordered mind, as well as a vivid imagination which never fails her. For Barbara Cartland to examine an idea in depth is for her to understand it, as she has a talent for thinking in the abstract — so much so that her powers of reasoning and abstraction often take place at the cost of directness and spontaneity. The thoughts follow each other with great rapidity, and the fact that she can think much faster than other people sometimes leads to outbursts of impatience and irritability.

Creative, enthusiastic and optimistic, she is able to develop ideas logically in her mind, and once those ideas begin to take on a form and a shape then it is very rare for the process to be disturbed by external influences.

Her heart rules her head, but there is a preference for direct action and forceful comment in defence of her views and opinions, and as there is great moral courage she will stoutly defend her beliefs, the strongest of which is the belief in the Divine Power of Life's work. She is greatly influenced by the strength of her will, and there is a disciplined control of the feelings and impulses so that she is able successfully to regulate the energies of her mind. Eager to get down to the essentials of a subject, and having, in addition, the ability to separate the important from the unimportant, she displays much efficiency in her work. The outlook is independent and the nature self-reliant so that she tends to remain unruffled when others panic.

Work and duty come before amusement, and creative satisfaction is given precedence over rest and relaxation, but in spite of this apparently ruthless pursuit of her aims she is ethically beyond reproach. She has a need to express her convictions and does what she believes is right, regardless of the consequences. Generally, there is an equanimity born of steadfastness which means that she is rarely if ever influenced in a way that would make her act against her better judgement.

Barbara Cartland is a socially desirable person who prefers not to deviate too far from the paths of convention, and this attitude has contributed much to the fulfilment of her many ambitions. Nevertheless she loves the unfamiliar and the unusual and there is a liking for tasks that really stretch her imagination and use to the full her creativity.

Possessing a subtle mind, she loves people as a whole, and enjoys meeting strangers the world over, but her love for her family takes precedence over everything else. Her private life has always been most important and the slogan in her home, 'My family first'. Her children, and her husband before he died, are the centre round which her whole life revolves.

Natural and unpretentious, her behaviour is the same whatever the occasion, whether she is spotlighted in the glare of publicity or quietly enjoying a relaxed moment at home with those she knows well.

It is quite clear from the strength of the handwriting that the dreaming spires of Barbara Cartland are securely built on the rock-like foundations of her character.

'Completely true' — Barbara Cartland